THE WHITE DRESS

Harriet Worsley

Laurence King Publishing

LAURENCE KING

Published in 2009 by
Laurence King Publishing Ltd.
361–373 City Road
London EC1V 1LR
United Kingdom
Tel: + 44 20 7841 6900
Fax: + 44 20 7841 6910
email: enquiries@laurenceking.com
www.laurenceking.com

A catalogue record for this book is available from the
British Library

ISBN-13: 978 1 85669 560 2

Printed in China

Designed by & SMITH

Acknowledgements
An enormous thank you to Jamie Lindsay
for his excellent eye, practical help and wise advice.
Thanks also to Rachel Carrington of *Hello!* magazine,
James Lever and Harriet Carr.

For my goddaughter Poppy Thomas

THE WHITE DRESS

CONTENTS

INTRODUCTION

This is the story of the wedding dress, from 1900 to the present day, told in ten exciting chapters. Taking themes such as Colour, Ritual and Goddess, each chapter examines different aspects of what a bride wears on her big day. Colour looks at the reasons why women have not always married in white. Ritual discusses wedding traditions and how they affect what women marry in today. The Goddess chapter celebrates the glamorous Hollywood bias-cut dress. And while focusing on the Western wedding dress, this book incidentally gives a history of twentieth-century fashion. To most women, the wedding dress is the best dress they will wear in their lives, and this story chronicles the collision between ordinary women and high fashion.

The history of wedding dresses and wedding rituals in this book will fascinate future brides and bridalwear designers. But *The White Dress* also focuses on contemporary bridal style. The superb photographs will inspire brides and designers either for their own wedding day or for their clients. There are no pictures of fashion disasters in *The White Dress*. This is a book for stylish brides about stylish brides, and each picture should serve as an inspiration.

Wherever possible, we will feature images of real women getting married, in a real context. Movie stills help our story along, showing some of the most glamorous bridal attire of each decade. And equally important are celebrity marriages: the actresses, singers and society beauties, from Bianca Jagger in St Tropez in a white suit to Princess Grace demure in white lace.

This is not only the story of the white wedding dress, but the escape from it, and in some respects, the liberation of women. Women have a love-hate relationship with the wedding dress –

Right

Jessica Simpson marries Nick Lachey in Austin, Texas in 2002. Crystals and pearls cover her elegant Vera Wang dress, giving a feminine opulence to the simple strapless ball gown.

that frequently overpriced, over-elaborate meringue so yearned after and, in reality so feared. No matter how beautiful and fascinating the story, it has always attempted to tell certain fictions about women. Women in the UK have only had the vote since 1918, and even then only women aged over thirty. Most wedding traditions developed long before women won such significant rights. Today the role of the bride in many traditional ceremonies is stereotypically submissive and virginal. There are still many contradictions. The Christian bride no longer has to pledge to obey her husband, but often wants to wear a virginal veil. She is still walked down the aisle by her father, and handed into the care of her husband, even if she is a thirty-five-year-old company director. She expects to be proposed to and to be given a fat diamond ring on engagement, even though she may earn more than her husband. Wedding rituals and traditions are always in a state of flux, but never more so than today, when women can at last play an equal part. And who knows what the future may hold?

The White Dress charts the loosening up of the constraints which a wedding dress represents, and the changes in public expectations of what a wedding should entail. Today it is less of a rite of passage, and more an orgy of consumerism. It is interesting to note that at the beginning of the century the white wedding dress and a lavish ceremony was the sole privilege of the rich. Those who could not afford such extravagance wore a best dress of any colour. In 1950, the average cost of a wedding, in today's terms, was £600. Now it is nearer £18,000, about thirty times more costly. The bridal industry is booming. This substantial sum could be used as a deposit on a flat, but brides and grooms choose to spend it on a dress, a party and a honeymoon. As the divorce rate in America for first-time marriages is approximately forty percent, some could argue that rising wedding costs now serve as insurance premium against splitting up. Is it getting a little out of control?

This book is also a history of a changing ritual, which takes its inspiration from an increasingly wide and exciting palette. Women do not always confine themselves simply to the dress that is worn to church. They want to get married in more than one outfit, and ceremonies can last a whole day, or even a weekend. We will examine the relationship between the formal, white wedding dress and its related eveningwear, and even touch on the Gretna Green wedding. As weddings become more bespoke and secular, so do the clothes. A woman might get married in a blue evening dress rather than

a full-length white gown. We also include some images from
same-sex weddings – what do two brides wear on their wedding
day? Although we are largely concerned with Western fashions,
we also cast an eye over the wedding costumes of other cultures.

With its strong narrative and judicious selection of fashion images,
The White Dress serves as an intelligent style bible for new brides
and bridalwear designers.

THE
FAIRYTALE
PRINCESS

She's said, 'Yes', there are stars in her eyes, there's a diamond on her finger and it's time for the fairytale to begin. A wedding is the big day that many women, and their mothers, dream about for decades. Suddenly it's not only about true love forever; invitations, flowers and tiaras have to be ordered and paid for. The well-oiled wheels of the wedding industry start whirring to realize the fantasy, with heart-shaped rice to throw and cream-carpeted showrooms bursting with hangers of silk and tulle. 'The Magic Begins Here…' promises the *House of Brides* website. But this magic world can also be intimidating, and expensive. The bride on her wedding day has to feel like the most beautiful woman in the room. The pressure is on.

Quite what it is that drives sane women, with simple tastes, into a complete Bridezilla frenzy, is a mystery. Peer pressure? Status? The bridal industry? Their mothers? *Brides* magazine in 2007 suggested that those planning an average wedding should budget for £3,698 for rings, wedding dress, going-away clothes, accessories and honeymoon wardrobe. Like little girls dressing up as fairies and ballerinas, this very public declaration of love can even sweep tomboys up into a frenzy of pearls, lace and Barbie-doll tulle. This may be the most expensive dress a woman ever buys, and extraordinarily, she may only wear it once. Her husband may never have seen her dressed like this before, and will probably never do so again. It is frighteningly more like theatre than real life. The bridal industry catches engaged women by the scruff of their necks, at a particularly vulnerable time, and gives them the hard sell. The underlying message is – without the perfect dress, you might not achieve the perfect marriage. 'With jeans as well as cars, we now are buying so much more than the object or artefact. We are buying into the imagery that surrounds the object,' writes Alan Thomlinson in *Consumption, Identity and Style*. With a dress, brides are buying a dream.

Tiaras, trains and a dress that was only worn once used to be the preserve of royalty and the aristocracy. When Queen Victoria married her first cousin Prince Albert in 1840, she endorsed the white wedding dress as the status symbol for brides who could afford it. She was seen as a modern romantic who married for love, in an ornate lace dress which was simpler than was usual for a Royal. At the turn of the century normal girls got married in their

Right

Here comes the bride. The photographers go wild as former Hartnell model Jane McNeil arrives at the church in Edinburgh in 1953, for her wedding to the Earl of Dalkeith.

Left

British designer John Galliano designed this spectacular dress for the Christian Dior Spring/ Summer 2007 Couture collection.

Sunday best, while the very rich might marry in a Paris dress by Charles Frederick Worth, the founding father of couture. One Worth dress could cost more than a working man's annual salary at the time. With photography, grand weddings went public, and by the Thirties ordinary women were starting to long for a lavish wedding of their own.

'Couturiers are the last possessors of the wand of Cinderella's fairy godmother,' said Christian Dior. But today anyone can buy crowns and ball gowns on the Internet, and brides from every walk of life can look like a storybook princess. Today's fairytale princess brides are rock and royalty: Victoria and David Beckham on their matching thrones in 1999, Princess Diana with her twenty-five-foot court train, and Mariah Carey in ivory silk Vera Wang and a diamond tiara. They've got the cash, they've got the status and they can give the public, and *Hello!* magazine, what it expects: glitz, crowns and thrones. There is naturally no need for over the top vulgarity. Princess Grace of Monaco, both princess and movie star, looked demure but sensational at her 1956 wedding, and pop star Gwen Stefani got it right in Dior by John Galliano. The ball gown wedding dress is the romantic's favourite in the West – a tightly-fitted bodice that explodes into a billowing skirt. Embroidery, pearls, crystal beads and lace are often used as detailing. And the fairytale would not be complete without a tiara, a cathedral train and veil, a fleet of bridesmaids and a cascade bouquet. Modern ball gown dresses are often strapless, as bare arms and shoulders are now more acceptable during a ceremony. Dresses today are sleeker, and without frills and flounces. But the ball gown is still a sign of affluence and the most traditional choice for a bride. The beading and embroidery are labour intensive and expensive. Big, layered skirts mean that the fabric alone can cost a small fortune. All this helps to keep country dressmakers and Paris couture houses in business today, as a wedding day is probably the only time in her life a woman would even consider a made-to-measure dress.

The Victorian and Edwardian influences on wedding dresses came and went during the 20th century. The 1939 film *Gone with the Wind*, with its 1860s style dresses, re-ignited a passion for Victoriana and gave birth to a host of wannabe Scarlett O'Hara brides in crinolines, bustles and leg o'mutton sleeves. With the outbreak of the Second World War, Europe swiftly enforced a streamlined silhouette, and many Americans felt it their duty to tone down lavish gowns. It took Christian Dior's New Look collection of 1947 to re-introduce

Europeans to evening and wedding dresses that scandalously used up to twenty-five yards of fabric. Waist cinchers created tiny torsos and stiff crinolines gave volume to wide mid-calf ballerina skirts. Nancy Mitford wrote in *Letters*, 'Have you heard about the New Look? You pad your hips & squeeze your waist & skirts are to the ankle it is bliss. So then you feel romantic like Mme Greffulhe & people shout ordures at you from vans because for some reason it creates class feeling in a way no sables could.' Brides added long veils, grand chapel or cathedral trains, lace, pearls, sequins and beading. While society girls patronized the Paris couture houses of Christian Dior and Cristóbal Balenciaga, bridalwear shops catered for the less well-heeled. The 1980s was all about thinking big. After the more streamlined Sixties and Seventies, women craved volume. They wanted silk and taffeta, boned bodices, ballooning sleeves and wide skirts over petticoats. Low necklines called for pearl chokers, or dresses were high-necked and Edwardian-inspired.

In Europe and the USA, deciding to get married today can be the most conventional choice that a woman ever makes, when she can live with a man and have his children without marriage. Many brides choose uncharacteristically traditional dresses – the epitome of this is the ball gown with its corsets and impractical swishing petticoated skirts. This is what Victorian women wore; women who often didn't work and couldn't vote, and were viewed as chattels of men. This dress style emphasizes the breasts and hips, suggesting voluptuous fertility, hearth and home – not independence. After working during the war, Fifties women were expected to go back to the home and reclaim their roles as wives and mothers, and Dior's wide-skirted womanly New Look reflected this. Women felt romantic. Marriage statistics boomed. During the Eighties, despite wearing power suits in the boardrooms, women chose nostalgic Victorian-style dresses as brides, suggesting that away from work traditional values still held. Today hearth and home are not the sole values of a twenty-first-century Western working woman, yet many brides marry in ball gowns. Family pressure, the bridal industry or just pure romance may twist the arm of a bride who lives in jeans and never thought she would turn overnight, like Cinderella, into a fairytale princess. When Jordan (aka Katie Price) married Peter André, she arrived in a glass Cinderella coach pulled by white horses with pink plumes. But the question is, what happens after the fairytale wedding is over? Mariah Carey, now divorced, commented on the MTV website: 'The dress was worn for a moment. And that moment was not an unhappy experience. It was the rest of the relationship that was the problem.'

Left

Esther Williams, swimming champion and movie star, shows a bit of leg in 1952. Her all-American good looks and athletic stature helped her Hollywood career blossom.

QUEEN ALEXANDRA AS A BRIDE
PAINTED IN 1863 BY LEUCHERT

Above

Princess Alexandra, daughter of Christian IX of Denmark and consort of Prince Edward, later King Edward VII, wears her wedding dress in this 1863 painting by Leuchert. The veil softens her dress and, draped around her shoulders, it takes on the appearance of a shawl or stole.

Left

Fashion editor Diana Vreeland included Catherine the Great's wedding dress (originally worn under a jewel encrusted silver lace cloak) in a 1976 New York exhibition. Catherine the Great overthrew her husband Peter III to become Empress of Russia.

Previous left

Chloe Delevingne marries Louis Buckworth in 2007 in London. Her strapless dress by Anouska Hempel is streamlined and simple, and typical of today's toned down take on the ball dress.

Above

Thalia, twenty-eight, marries Tommy Mottola, fifty-two, in 2000. Mitzy designed the Latin pop princess's dress with its seventeen-metre train. Her blusher veil draws attention to the pretty off-the-shoulder neckline.

Previous right

Actress Audrey Hepburn poses for the camera in 1954. Long white gloves and ball gown dresses were de rigueur for brides in the 1950s.

Above

Andalusian design duo Victorio & Lucchino cleverly use flowers to puff up a sleeve of this romantic white wedding dress in 2006. The Victorians often festooned dresses with real orange blossom – a symbol of fertility and everlasting love.

Right

Actress Joan Crawford wears a romantic dress by MGM costume designer Adrian for the 1932 film *Letty Lynton*. The dress was soon imitated and helped to fuel a trend for wide shoulders and sleeves. 1930s summer brides sometimes wore garden frocks in chiffon or organza in place of the usual slinky bias-cut wedding dress.

Prince Rainier of Monaco took the movie star Grace Kelly as his princess and bride in 1956. Her dress, by MGM head costume designer Helen Rose, featured a rose point lace bodice, a silk faille bell-shaped skirt and seed pearl detailing.

Above

In 1984 pop princess Madonna shot to worldwide fame with *Like a Virgin* and caused a sensation by writhing about on a giant wedding cake at the MTV Video Music Awards wearing an irreverent wedding gown.

Legendary couturier Christian Dior, who invented the 'New Look' and the 'A-line', poses with six of his models wearing strapless ball dresses after a fashion show at the Savoy Hotel, London in 1950.

Right

Princess Alexandra, daughter of Christian IX of Denmark and consort of Prince Edward, later King Edward VII, is shown here painted by Leuchert in her wedding dress in 1863.

The legendary society photographer Cecil Beaton took this striking photograph of Princess Margaret. Norman Hartnell designed many of Princess Margaret's dresses for official engagements and society events.

Above

In this 1951 wedding portrait of Queen Soraya and Shah Mohammed Reza Pahlavi, commonly known as the Last Shah of Iran, the bride wears a silver lamé pearl-studded dress designed by Christian Dior. The wedding took place at Golestan Palace in Tehran.

Above

Rolling Stones guitarist Ronnie Wood celebrates with fellow Stones Charlie Watts and Keith Richards after marrying Jo Howard in 1985.

Right

Blonde bombshell Jayne Mansfield and her actor and body builder husband Mickey Hargitay marry at Rancho Palos Verdes, California, in 1958. The actress was tragically killed in a car crash aged only thirty-four.

Above

A model in Paris in 1953 wears a wedding dress by Hubert de Givenchy. Fifties low-cut dresses could be transformed into suitably modest bridalwear with the addition of a cropped spencer jacket or a sheer lace over-blouse.

Right

A model shows off a wedding dress on the Paris catwalk from the Elie Saab couture Spring/Summer 2006 collection. The lavish surface detailing gives this classic ball gown dress a dash of opulence and sophistication.

Left

Twenty-four-year-old Jacqueline Bouvier dances with her husband John F. Kennedy on their wedding day at Rhode Island in 1953. Her dress was made of fifty metres of ivory silk taffeta, and covered in tiny wax flowers. It took dressmaker Ann Lowe two months to make.

Above

Queen Victoria marries at the Chapel Royal St James's Palace in 1840. She endorsed the white wedding dress and was celebrated for her low-key romantic attire – natural orange blossom instead of a tiara and simple lace rather than fabric laden with jewels.

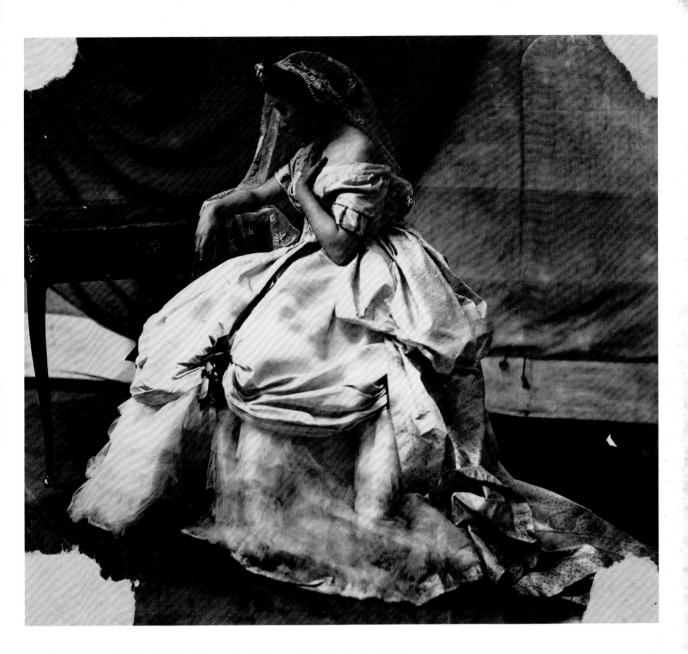

Left

Model Shalom Harlow is British
fashion designer John Galliano's
geisha bride at the Christian Dior
Spring/Summer 2007 haute
couture show.

Above

The pioneering British photographer
Lady Clementina Hawarden dresses up
as an eighteenth-century shepherdess
for this 1860s photograph.

Above

Isabel Goldsmith, daughter of entrepreneur James Goldsmith, marries Baron Arnaud de Rosnay in 1973. The flowers in her hair and her soft chignon cleverly complement the detail on the bodice and the rounded leg o'mutton sleeves.

Previous left

Movie star Ginger Rogers goes for full romance as a bride in white in 1938, with a fashionable headdress and her hair rolled back to frame the face.

Right

English rose. HRH Princess Victoria and a fellow bridesmaid sit for a photographer in 1893 at the wedding of the future Queen Mary and King George V. Pale pink roses accessorize the white satin dresses with their chiffon sleeves.

Previous right

Simonetta Stefanelli plays the bride Apollonia Vitelli Corleone in Francis Ford Coppola's 1972 film *The Godfather*. Shortly afterwards her character is killed by a car bomb destined for her new husband.

Left

Joan Rivers poses with the newlyweds Melissa Rivers and John Endicott at the New York City Trump Plaza in 1998. The bride's Vera Wang duchesse satin dress is detailed with embroidery and sparkling crystals.

Above

Quick getaway. Angie Everhart runs out of a Beverly Hills church after her marriage to Ashley Hamilton in 1996. The double-tier scalloped hem of her dress adds detail and interest to the plain skirt.

Above

Elton John marries Renate Blauel
in Sydney in 1984. With its high
frilled Edwardian-style neckline, and
ballooning leg o'mutton sleeves, the
diamond-studded wedding dress
reflects the Eighties enthusiasm for
volume and opulence.

Right

This layered net evening dress was
designed by Julian Rose, and modelled
by Barbara Goalen in 1950. It could
easily pass for a twenty-first-century
wedding dress. Brides in the 1950s
often covered up their shoulders with
lace, but today it is more acceptable
for brides to go bare. The layered
fabric creates an illusion of a larger
bust, while emphasizing the tiny waist,
which would have been pulled in
by a strapless waist-pincher.

NO FUSS, NO FRILLS

No fuss, no frills – just plain, simple elegance. Some of the most stylish brides of the twentieth century have rejected fairytale frills for clean, unembellished minimalism. Ambitious but revolutionary Coco Chanel pioneered the sleek boyish look of the Roaring Twenties, where women cut their hair into short Eton crops and wore dresses which ignored the hips. It was dubbed the 'Garçonne' look, from the censored French novel *La Garçonne*, which chronicled the antics of sexually liberated, short-haired career women. Chanel introduced daringly short streamlined 1920s wedding dresses worn with court trains, and confirmed that white was the only colour for self-respecting brides. So women walked down the aisle in sleeveless little white or ivory shifts, with dropped waists, skirts above the calf, and satin festooned with rhinestones, crystals, sequins, beads and pearls. Couturier Lucile wrote in her book *Discretions and Indiscretions*, 'It brought in the ideal of the "boyish woman". Here was the perfect solution to the problem. Slight figures covered with three yards of material, skirt ending just below the knees, tiny cloche hat trimmed with a band of ribbon. No woman, at least no woman in civilisation, could cost less to clothe! And best of all the women were delighted.' Women from all social classes could afford this new style of dress. Chanel said: 'Women should dress as plainly as their maids.' And the vogue for costume jewellery (another Chanel innovation) meant that maids could sparkle as brightly as a duchess. It was about time. These easy wedding dresses were feather-light and highly practical compared to the restrictive Victorian ball gowns of thirty years earlier. They reflected the new-found emancipation of women. When they were required to work in the factories and the farms during the First World War, their dress naturally became more utilitarian. And finally, in 1918, women over thirty got the vote in the UK.

Simplicity surfaced again during the Second World War. 1940s American brides toned down their nineteenth-century-style white dresses, as to look too lavishly dressed was considered unpatriotic. UK brides had much less choice. However, lace and furnishing fabrics were not restricted by rationing and coupons, and became useful for making white dresses; women even used parachute silk when they could get hold of it. But weddings often had to be arranged in great haste, to seize the opportunity when the men were briefly home. By far the most practical and elegant option

Right

Actress Sharon Tate marries film director Roman Polanski, 1968. Designer Mary Quant launched schoolgirl mini dresses from her Kings Road shop in the Sixties, and they became a symbol of that decade. Tiny flowers or ribbons in the hair became a fashionable alternative to a veil at the time.

for women was a streamlined Utility suit with its tight skirt and neat jacket, commissioned by the British Board of Trade to be in line with the new fabric restrictions. Both Norman Hartnell and Hardy Amies designed a version. By the end of the war each British adult was allowed thirty-six clothing coupons a year. A Utility suit could be bought for eighteen coupons. As land was used for growing food rather than flowers, there were few bouquets, but brides pinned fabric flowers into their hair or onto their suits as corsages.

When ex-civil engineer André Courrèges launched his minimal 1964 Space Age collection in a white and chrome showroom, it set the tone for the decade. His simple geometric dresses cut in heavy fabric that hung away from the body looked startlingly new because they were so simple. 1964 *Vogue* advised: 'Girls with a positive outlook go for clear-cut effects.' Mary Quant borrowed from the slick tailoring of the mods, for short childlike gymslips, and women were quick to reject the voluptuous maternal silhouettes of the Fifties. There were paper wedding dresses, clean-cut mini dresses and beanie hats covered in fabric for the veil-less bride. Ornamentation was out. Formal wedding dresses in the early Sixties were like monks' robes, with minimal seams, bell sleeves, and bodices that flowed straight into skirts with no apparent waistline. Even the Royal Family followed. Princess Margaret's 1960 wedding dress by Norman Hartnell, despite its wide skirt and tiny waist, was executed in understated silk organza with none of the usual beading or lace.

After the indulgent Eighties, with its bouffant skirts and brash logos, the purist 1990 New Age white collection by Rifat Ozbek, and simple Nineties luxury from Jil Sander and Zoran were the perfect antidote. 'In Winter, it's all-over white. Worn head-to-toe or in graded shades of blonde, it's modern, uplifting and part of a bold, brilliant new world,' suggested British *Vogue* in 1994. As always, bridalwear was three steps behind, as even those who wanted silk pyjamas and cashmere T-shirts for normal daywear went operatic for their wedding. It took Vera Wang, ex-*Vogue* editor and former design director at Ralph Lauren, to change this by launching a bridal collection in 1994. Her dresses were shockingly simple, understated, elegant and quite unlike the Lady Di dress. She reputedly said, 'When I first showed my dresses, people walked out.' Simple is a timelessly stylish option. Carolyn Bessette

Kennedy married in 1996 in a plain slip dress designed by Narciso Rodriguez, and Denise Richards chose a Giorgio Armani plain silk slip as Charlie Sheen's bride in 2002.

The white suit – with trousers or a skirt – is a sleek modern option for brides who cannot contemplate the idea of wearing a dress. In the 1930s Marlene Dietrich, the bisexual film goddess, invited shocked reactions by openly wearing trouser suits and was nicknamed 'the best dressed man in Hollywood'. Yves Saint Laurent slipped a couple of satin-lapelled trouser suits into his 1966 collection. The next year he made his 'Le Smoking' trouser suit the focus of his collection. It set a trend. Saint Laurent said in *Vogue* in 1969, 'I finally got women into jersey, out of bras and into pants.' Even then, a trouser suit was still a daring, modern option for formal occasions, but fashionable brides and grooms embraced it with his-and-her matching white trouser suits for civil weddings. '*Elle* magazine ran article after article on Yves Saint Laurent and his *Smokings*, but it wouldn't let its own journalists wear trousers to work. Imagine!' exclaimed Parisian art director Maïmé Arnodin (in *Yves Saint Laurent* by Alice Rawsthorn).

If you want to make an impact as a bride, then try pared-down simplicity. And, in the words of the great fashion doyenne Diana Vreeland, always remember: 'Elegance is refusal.'

Right

Joe DiMaggio and Marilyn Monroe kiss after their marriage ceremony in 1954. A tailored suit was appropriate for a civil service, and the white collar frames the face and highlights the sex symbol's blonde curls.

Denise Richards marries actor Charlie
Sheen in Los Angeles in 2002. They
both wear clothes by designer Giorgio
Armani. Richard's minimalist satin
slip dress was teamed with a jacket
beaded with shimmering crystals.

Above

Marla Maples marries tycoon Donald
Trump in 1993 in New York. The low
neckline of her dress by Carolina Herrera
emphasizes her impressive cleavage.

Left

Pop legend Lulu marries Maurice Gibb of The Bee Gees in Buckinghamshire, England, in 1969. Her long white mink-trimmed coat covers a white silk mini dress. Hoods, scarves and bonnets became fashionable during the Sixties as an alternative to the traditional veil.

Previous left

Actress Mia Farrow ties the knot with Frank Sinatra in Las Vegas in 1966. The simplicity of the boxy dress and matching cropped jacket works perfectly with her gamine good looks and closely cut hair.

Above

Actress Talitha Pol marries playboy John Paul Getty Jr in 1966 in Rome. She wore a white mink-trimmed mini. The style icon and sometime muse of Yves Saint Laurent died of an overdose in 1971.

Previous right

Beatle Paul McCartney weds American photographer Linda Eastman in 1969. She wears a yellow coat over a fawn dress, and is accompanied by her daughter Heather.

Above

Lord Digby escorts his daughter Pamela to her 1939 wedding to Randolph Churchill, the Conservative politician and son of Winston Churchill. Her dark wartime wedding outfit makes the perfect backdrop for her pale bouquet.

Right

Natalie Wood and Robert Wagner leave the church in Arizona after their wedding in 1957. Her hooded lace cropped jacket cleverly serves as a veil while modestly covering her shoulders for the ceremony.

Above

Movie star Judy Garland marries Vicente Minnelli in 1945. The fashionable wide shoulders of her dress emphasize her tiny waist.

Left

Nineteen-year-old screen starlet Ava Gardner marries Mickey Rooney in 1942 in California. Her skirt-suit and coloured veil is an elegant sartorial option for a small and simple wedding. During the Second World War corsages replaced bouquets, many women married in suits, and even in America it was seen as unpatriotic to wear a lavish white wedding dress.

Right

Style icon Audrey Hepburn poses for the camera in a boatneck evening dress. The sash breaks up the sea of white, and her outfit would be perfect for a bride today looking for a clean-cut formal wedding dress. Long white gloves are rarely worn today, but were popular with brides until the early Sixties.

Previous left

Princess Margaret leaves Westminster Abbey with her new husband Antony Armstrong-Jones in 1960. Her dress, designed by Norman Hartnell, was understated for a Royal with none of the usual beading and embroidery. The silk organza ball gown has a V-cut neckline and a skirt flung wide with layers of petticoats.

Previous right

Priscilla Beaulieu ties the knot in Las Vegas with Elvis Presley in 1967. Her white silk chiffon dress was festooned with seed pearls. Sixties wedding dresses had become almost monkishly plain. They often had no defined waist and dropped straight to the floor from the shoulders.

Sex kitten Brigitte Bardot plays the bride in white in 1957. When she married Jacques Charrier in 1959 she chose designer Jacques Esterel to make her a low-key dress in pink and white checked linen trimmed with broderie anglaise. It set a trend for pink gingham.

Above

Claudia Schiffer models for Chanel in 1995. The classic Chanel jacket is seen here tightened and elongated to form a streamlined elegant wedding dress.

British actor David Niven is photographed at his wedding to Swedish model Hjordis Tersmeden in 1948. The bride's corsage worn on her dark skirt-suit is a fashionable alternative to a bouquet.

Bianca Jagger strides through Heathrow Airport in a white three-piece suit, black bowler hat and carrying a cane in 1972. A tailored white suit is an option for a bride looking for a sharper alternative to the white dress.

THE
GODDESS

A bride on her wedding day is put up on a pedestal, treated like a goddess, and expected to dress like one. What then could be more glamorous than a full-length bias-cut red carpet dress, the threads clinging to every curve? Paul Poiret opened his Paris couture house in 1903, and with Jeanne Paquin at the House of Paquin, persuaded women to shed their whalebone corsets so they could emerge like colourful butterflies wearing the new empire line. While the suffragettes chained themselves to railings and fought for the vote, the fashionable flitted free in dresses falling in folds from a 'waistline' under the bust. Classical drapery influenced Mariano Fortuny who constructed minutely pleated Delphos gowns, tied to the body with a silk cord and weighted with Murano glass beads. Off the body, they reduced down to a twist of coloured silk. Ancient Greece became an obsession, fleetingly, and the fashionable married in white Delphos gowns. In ancient Rome brides had worn brand new white tunics, with a wool cord fastened with the Knot of Hercules – for the bridegroom to untie. When Madeleine Vionnet opened her couture house in Paris in 1912, she took up the baton and invented the bias-cut dress. She masterfully draped, gathered and twisted the fabric so that it flowed over the body like water.

The stock market crashed in 1929, and ordinary women escaped the grim reality of the Depression by dreaming of fairytale weddings with all the trimmings. But only the rich could afford them. To sell the dream a new magazine was launched in 1934 called *So You're Going to Be Married!*. It became *Brides*. The mesmeric glamour of Hollywood provided instant escapism. Actresses became international superstars almost overnight, and women religiously copied the hats, haircuts and shimmering evening dresses of Joan Crawford, Marlene Dietrich and Greta Garbo. The Hollywood costume designers, Travis Banton at Paramount Pictures and Gilbert Adrian at MGM, made sure that the sirens of the silver screen always dressed meticulously, on and off camera.

The Thirties marked the birth of the long, white bias-cut dress. By the close of the 1920s the boyish silhouette had softened and, once again, dresses started to trace the female figure. Suddenly it was all about high gloss and high glamour. When Princess Marina of Greece married in 1934, she wore a much-copied bias-cut dress by Edward Molyneux, with a draped neckline and long medieval

Right

Star of the silver screen Bette Davis poses for the camera. The plunging back and belt clasp of her dress create an elegant drama. Low-backed evening dresses in the 1930s were cut perfectly to show off a deep suntan. For a wedding ceremony, the back view of the bride must always be considered as she may be facing away from her guests.

sleeves. Her diamond tiara, fringed like the sun's rays, helped to bring diadems back into fashion. Wedding dresses in white high-sheen rayon, jersey and satin skimmed the figure and flared out from the knee, revealing every lump, bump and curve. To give the illusion of extra height, the fabric poured over the feet and spilled onto the floor. Worn with long flowing veils, and girdled at the waist, the dresses transformed brides into alluringly glamorous medieval sirens. Bridalwear followed eveningwear trends, but at parties women showed more skin, with plunging necklines and swooping backs in white satin and black velvet. Designer Madame Grès borrowed references from Eastern drapery with its wrapped and draped Indian dhotis and saris. The draped and ruched bodices complemented fashionable softly-waved hair. The look was simple, sexy and body skimming; and beautifully accessorized by the glint and sparkle of diamanté on sun-kissed skin.

Bias-cut draped dresses came back into fashion in the 1970s, with the birth of disco, the expertise of American designer Halston, and the patronage of the cocaine-fuelled 'catpack' who danced till dawn at Studio 54. Halston dressed Bianca Jagger, Liza Minnelli and Jackie Onassis in luxurious evening dresses of loosely draped jersey and satin. But it wouldn't do for the wedding day as these dresses just looked too sexy. Seventies brides remained more traditional, preferring loosely frilled nostalgic dresses rather than starlet-style draped satin gowns. Halston's dresses would be much more suitable for brides today who are happy to take red-carpet style to the altar. Long bias-cut wedding dresses in an evening dress style are becoming popular with brides who want to party into the night after the ceremony. Zac Posen is renowned for his bias-cut dresses. Gowns by Collette Dinnigan, Amanda Wakeley, Catherine Walker, Badgley Mischka, Jenny Packham and Rebecca Street are all good choices for brides looking for glamour. John Galliano is the master of the modern bias cut today, and his bespoke wedding dresses under his own label or at Dior, where he is artistic director, should turn most Cinderellas into Goddesses. For a price, of course. In 2006, Sophia Kokosalaki designed the first clothing collection for the reopened House of Vionnet since it pulled down the shutters in 1939. Marc Audibet took the reins as artistic advisor in 2008. So the legacy of Madame Vionnet, the mistress of the bias cut, lives on.

Left

Actress Drew Barrymore wears a diaphanous dress by John Galliano for Christian Dior in 2007.

Right

Beach belle. This Amanda Wakeley jersey wedding dress with its Swarovski beaded straps would be ideal for a bride marrying on the beach.

Previous left

An elegant bride storms the catwalk at the Giorgio Armani Spring/Summer 2007 couture show. The jewelled band is cleverly integrated into the dress, and the opaque matching veil almost serves as a second train.

Previous right

Supermodel Kate Moss looks like a 1930s screen goddess at The Golden Age of Couture Gala in London in 2007. Her pale gold bias-cut silk dress complements her long blonde hair.

Left

Barbara Stanwyck wears a glamorous evening dress that could easily be worn by a bride today. The draped sash detailing and defined shoulders create a stunning back view.

Above

Bette Davis is every inch the sex symbol with her second-skin white dress. Bias-cut white dresses in silk and satin, which showed every curve, were favourites of 1930s starlets, and would suit lithe, body-confident brides today.

Left

Newlywed singer and dancer Josephine Baker, who was nicknamed Black Venus and Black Pearl, cuts a dash in a grand hat at her wedding in Millandes, France in 1947.

Previous left

A model on the catwalk at the Dior fashion show in Prague in 2007 shows off a sleek ruched dress with an ornate beaded front panel. Brides who want to keep jewellery simple can introduce glitter and glitz using beading and embroidery on the bodice of their dress.

Above

Edwina Ashley marries Lord Louis Mountbatten, great-grandson of Queen Victoria, in 1922 in London. Her silver dress by London fashion house Reville-Terry was decorated with trailing stole panels embroidered in crystal and diamanté.

Previous right

Starlet Betty Grable strikes a pose in 1942. Her sheer lace overdress tones down the sexy white gown underneath. Brides who want to look demure for the ceremony can choose lace coats, overdresses or tight jackets over their strapless dress.

Left

Marlene Dietrich, the bisexual screen
actress, notorious for her shockingly
masculine trouser suits, here looks
every inch the woman in her long
white dress. Milliners such as Philip
Treacy brought feathered headpieces
back into fashion in the 1990s, and
they became popular for wedding
guests and brides as an alternative
to a wide-brimmed hat or veil.

Right

Draped necklines and dresses which
spilled over the feet and onto the floor
were 1930s tricks that helped to soften
the face, complement the fashionable
waved hair and give the impression
of added height.

Previous left

This long wedding dress by Yves
Saint Laurent for Spring/Summer
1999 is reminiscent of dresses from
ancient Greece and Rome. Its empire
line emphasizes the décolletage, and
the flowers in the hair are a neat
replacement for a veil.

Previous right

Russian Ballet dancer Anna Pavlova
lets loose and dances freely without
a corset. Her dress is similar to those
made by designer Mario Fortuny who
was famous for his pleated Delphos
gowns inspired by ancient Greece.

Right

Bette Davis wears a metallic goddess dress, with a low-cut back. A bride who wants to look sexy for the evening, but modest for the ceremony, could choose a daring low-backed dress with a matching stole.

Above

Supermodel Naomi Campbell wears Elie Saab haute couture for Autumn/Winter 2003–04 in Paris. Luxurious dresses in silver brocade and silver and gold lamé were popular for 1920s and 1930s brides.

Left

Yohji Yamamoto's Spring/Summer 1998 catwalk show explored the theme of marriage and included a bride and groom exchanging clothes. This classically twisted and draped wedding dress flows elegantly off the body.

Right

Actress Gwyneth Paltrow wears a silk satin Stella McCartney dress in 2005. This dress would work well for a bride having an evening wedding reception, as it combines high glamour with classy elegance.

Previous left

Lee Radziwill steps out on the town with dancer Rudolf Nureyev in New York in 1974. Her cobweb-light cape perfectly complements the simplicity of her simple white slip dress.

Previous right

Clark Gable and Constance Bennett raise their glasses in *After Office Hours* in 1934. The fluid butterfly sleeves of her dress cleverly follow the line of her waved hair.

Sex bomb Jean Harlow looks anything
but demure in this slippery white
halter-neck dress. Halter necks were
an important eveningwear trend in the
1930s and designer Madeleine Vionnet
promoted the look.

Right

Rita Hayworth smoulders seductively
in 1942. Dresses with fitted bodices
and fuller skirts came back into
fashion in the 1940s and the silhouette
became more extreme in 1947 with the
birth of Christian Dior's New Look.

Left

A bride and groom drink champagne after their wedding ceremony in Manhattan. The wide shoulders of her dress cleverly emphasize her slim figure.

Previous left

This Christian Dior bride strolls down the catwalk at the Autumn/Winter 2000–01 couture shows in Paris. Designer John Galliano is renowned for his long bias-cut dresses, and this wedding dress is pure 1930s Hollywood glamour.

Above

American film actress Carole Landis and her husband Thomas Wallace are toasted at the Savoy Hotel, London, in 1943. White dresses were a rare luxury during the thrifty war years in Britain. Most women married in suits or in uniform.

Previous right

Florence Crane marries in 1933 in Chicago. Her long glossy dress with its high neckline and sleeves cut long over the hands is typically 1930s.

Above

German designer Karl Lagerfeld takes a peek at his catwalk bride at the Chanel Spring/Summer 2007 couture show in Paris. His collection was inspired by Sixties wild child Edie Sedgwick.

Right

Hollywood movie star Joan Crawford poses in a diaphanous white dress, with an empire-line bodice and flowing train that would not look out of place at the altar today.

Left

The pretty blonde curls of actress Bette Davis are perfectly set off by the frilled detailing on her dress and jacket. Her cropped feminine jacket would make a perfect cover up when worn over a sexy evening dress.

Above

Society dressmaker Norman Hartnell designed this ostrich feather cape for Lady Alice Montagu-Douglas-Scott on her marriage to the Duke of Gloucester. It was a wedding present from the South African Government in 1935.

Left

Jean Harlow shows a bit of leg in her magnificent white bias-cut evening dress with its lavish drapery. Loose and wide sleeves made a column dress look even longer and leaner.

Right

Actress Angelina Jolie looks timelessly elegant in a white dress by Marc Bouwer at the Oscars in Hollywood in 2004. The daring neckline, slashed to the waist, draws attention to her bold necklace.

Diva Diana Ross marries shipping tycoon Arne Naess in Switzerland in 1986. Her cream lace cape adds a feminine elegance to her whiter-than-white shimmering dress. Like a Twenties bride, the flowers in her hair sit at eye level rather than on the top of the head.

Right

Less is more. This strapless wedding dress by Vera Wang for 2007 is the epitome of timeless elegance. The gentle drapery on the bodice draws attention to the face, while the long skirt is simple but feminine.

A model wears a dress by designer Madeleine Vionnet in 1935. Vionnet invented the bias cut, and was famous for her classically inspired draped dresses that clung to the body's curves. She serves as an inspiration for designers today, notably John Galliano.

This pleated gold lamé dress is by Marc Audibet for the reopened House of Vionnet for Spring/Summer 2008. Madame Vionnet was famous for dressing the stars, particularly Greta Garbo and Marlene Dietrich, but she closed her Paris House in 1939 when war broke out.

THE DAMSEL

Fashion bounces back and forth between hard structural silhouettes and soft fluidity. The corseted bodices with their wide skirts at the turn of the century and the thick trapeze dresses hanging like shells away from the body in the Sixties did not last. There is always a softening, and a return to fluid romance. Languid white dresses, reminiscent of medieval maidens, are a constantly recurring motif. In the early 1900s, there was a vogue for medieval, Celtic and art nouveau detailing. By the Twenties, brides dressed like Lord Alfred Tennyson's Lady of Shalott, in white dresses with braided girdles and silver cords, flower garlands and deep medieval sleeves. For a more ethereal look, they wore light and airy overdresses embroidered with pearls and crystals. The late Queen Mother's wedding dress in 1923 drew inspiration from medieval Italy, with its bands of silver lamé criss-crossing a delicate bodice of chiffon moiré. With the Thirties came a new glamorous simplicity. Madeleine Vionnet designed a medieval Madonna dress, and brides drifted down the aisle in their medieval-style robes carrying bouquets of bright white Madonna lilies.

The damsel in distress, or the persecuted nubile maiden, was an archetypal character in medieval romances, where she was helpless until a knight-errant arrived on his shining charger to rescue her. It is a classic theme that runs through art and literature worldwide. But it is not a theme that empowers women in any way. The stereotypical damsel is weak and helpless until her man arrives. The pretty maid in her medieval-style dress and flowers in her hair is a recurring theme in bridal fashion and, unlike a white trouser suit, is still seen as a traditional and unchallenging choice in bridal dress.

Brides who want to get married in a simple, fluid and feminine dress often consider a contemporary empire-line gown. The 'waistline' sits high up under the bust, and skirts flow downward. Its origins are in ancient Greece and Rome, and it was famously adopted at the beginning of the 1800s by the deeply extravagant Empress Josephine, wife of Napoleon. An empire-line dress in white not only reflected high social status as it dirtied easily, but it also clung to the body in a racy way. Couturier Paul Poiret helped to bring the empire line back into fashion in the early 1900s.

Right

Norman Parkinson photographed model Jerry Hall wearing a wedding gown in this ornate bedroom at Versailles, France, in 1975. Seventies brides favoured loose dresses gathered at the waist with a fluid belt and long sleeves. They wore circlets of fresh flowers over flowing natural hair.

Béatrice Chatelier, third wife of
French record executive Eddie
Barclay, ties the knot in Paris
in 1970. Her wide-brimmed hat
and off-the-shoulder dress
present a less formal but very
feminine option for a summer
wedding.

Fast forward to the freewheeling Seventies and it's all about bra-burning and free love. And the empire line is back. Designers such as Zandra Rhodes, Bill Gibb, John Bates and Ossie Clark created flowing maxi dresses in lace and layered printed sheer fabric. There was a freedom about the empire line, with its swirling whirling skirts, that tied in with the easy hippie aesthetic of letting it all hang loose. Women embraced wide, long, flowing skirts, and borrowed from around the world – India, China and Afghanistan. Or they were seduced by the nostalgic pastoral look with white prairieland petticoats, epitomized by brands such as Laura Ashley in England. There was a wistful return to innocence, a looking back, and a complete rejection of the futuristic space-race aesthetic. Wedding dresses were long, lean and relaxed, and brides arrived at their weddings in horse-drawn traps. Sometimes the dresses had no defined waist, others were gathered in with a bow or belt. The more avant-garde went for the vintage look in 1920s beaded dresses. There were lace, chiffon or embroidered layered dresses with long sleeves. The feeling was filmy and light, like cobwebs dancing in the breeze. It was about unblemished maidens in embroidered smocks, with sweet-smelling wild flowers in their hair. And, let's face it, a complete fantasy.

By the mid-Seventies, the frills were back, with falling flounces draped around the body, full sleeves and frilled cuffs. It was as if the bones of the dresses had been removed, just leaving the slack skin hanging and drifting. Buns, chignons, high piles of ringlets or hair worn loose and long complemented the Seventies aesthetic. And rings of flowers or wide floppy hats were worn alongside tiaras and long veils.

The loose, unstructured damsel style works best today for informal summer, garden or beach weddings, or ceremonies with a daytime reception. A wide-brimmed hat or a ring of flowers are the obvious accessories. It's all about an easy youthful feminine simplicity, a world away from formal boned couture gowns. And there is now a crucial difference. Women may dress like damsels, but can quite happily take the reins themselves. They no longer have to wait helplessly for their knight to save them.

This streamlined simple dress by Oscar de la Renta relies on the fabric for its beautiful ornamentation. A truly modern dress, it has a minimal train, and could happily be dressed up with a veil, or left unadorned.

Right

London designer Ashley Isham's lace wedding dress with its bold pleated chiffon mermaid train was the dramatic final catwalk piece of his Autumn/Winter 2007–08 show.

When Princess Marina of Greece married her second cousin the Duke of Kent in 1934, she wore a much-copied bias-cut dress in white and silver brocade by designer Edward Molyneux. She helped to set the trend for a new medieval-style simplicity – tiaras fringed like sunrays, draped necklines and wide sleeves.

Above

Star of the silent screen, Billie Dove wears a wedding gown and headdress and holds a bouquet of lilies. Twenties brides favoured snug fitting headpieces or artificial flowers worn over each ear. Their long flowing tulle veils complemented the short boyish dresses fashionable at the time.

pure silk chiffon printed white on white fine fine pleats. tiny waist tied with satin band with lovely bow at back. Pearled, pleated frill above the waist.

Rhodes

Above

This 1972 wedding dress with its pleated white satin skirt and pale cream print is by Zandra Rhodes. The epaulettes are also edged with pleats. After short crisp mini dresses of the 1960s, the 1970s ushered in a new relaxed silhouette with loose frills and whirling skirts.

Right

A full-length romantic-style wedding dress by Jeanne Lanvin in ribbed voile is sleeveless and worn with a high waisted sash. A wide, floppy brimmed hat in the same material ties under the chin with a bow to match the sash.

Above

Songwriter Jim Webb stands with his bride Patsy Sullivan and their best man and bridesmaid during their wedding ceremony, which took place outdoors under a tree in 1974.

Previous left

Make-up artist Jemma Kidd and the Earl of Mornington marry at St James Church in Barbados. The bride wears a dress that looks both relaxed and romantic and is cleverly set off by an understated pink posy.

Right

The 1970s ushered in a new fluidity after the stiff monkish dresses of the Sixties. Loose frills, bands of lace and a return to historical references meant that brides were taking influences from country peasants and romantic Victoriana.

Previous right

Barefoot bride. Kenny Chesney kisses the hand of his new bride Renée Zellweger on a beach in the US Virgin Islands in 2005. Zellweger wore an understated wedding gown designed by Carolina Herrera.

Left

Crown Prince Haakon of Norway
and his wife Mette-Marit leave Oslo
Cathedral in 2001. Her four-year-old
son was a pageboy. The sculptural
white silk crepe dress was designed
by Ove Harder Finseth, and she
carried a trailing muff bouquet
of orchids, hydrangeas and roses.

Above

Pre-Raphaelite artist John William
Waterhouse painted the *Lady of Shalott*
in 1888, inspired by Alfred Tennyson's
poem. She brought a curse on herself
by looking directly at Sir Lancelot
and the blown-out candles here are
intended to suggest death. She wears
a long white medieval-style dress.

-185

Left

Hollywood actress Vilma Bánky plays the bride in George Fitzmaurice's screen version of *The Dark Angel*. A layer of lace covers the satin underdress, and she wears a corsage of orange blossom at the waist. A veil of white tulle flows from underneath a cap of rose point lace.

Above

The veil and train of a 1930s bride billows in the wind as she and her husband leave the church after their wedding. During the Thirties many dresses were accessorized with cathedral, court or sweep trains.

Above

Pete Townshend of British rock group
The Who marries Karen Astley in
1968. Her wide-sleeved romantic
dress takes its influences from the
Edwardian era, and shows how
wedding dresses became softer and
more fluid at the end of the Sixties.

Right

Actress Keira Knightley wears a
Sixties-style dress in 2007. The more
daring brides in the 1960s chose
short pin-tucked or gymslip dresses
which hung away from the body
in flowery lace, or fabric covered
with embroidery.

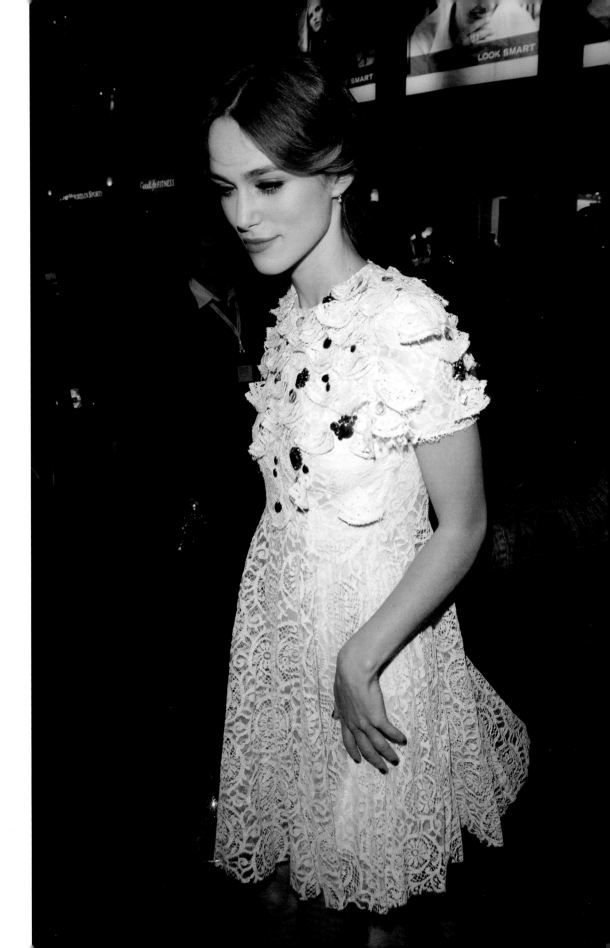

Left

A bride in 1912 gets ready for her wedding. Headdresses at the time were sometimes covered in pearls and wax flowers. Silk flowers or rosettes were often fastened to high empire waistlines.

Above

Bobby Gillespie, Primal Scream frontman, marries fashion stylist Katy England in Staffordshire in 2006. Her pink and white striped dress by Alexander McQueen and wild flower bouquet look natural and romantic, and perfectly suited to an English mid-summer country wedding.

Mrs Ronald Lambert is pictured wearing a white satin gown and a magnificent veil of Honiton lace for her wedding in 1920. Simple boyish 1920s dresses needed long ornate veils as contrasting accessories. Her ballerina shoes have pretty ribbon cross straps at the ankle.

Above

Lady Elizabeth Bowes-Lyon, the late Queen Mother, marries the future King George VI in 1923. Court dressmaker Madame Handley Seymour designed her medieval-style wedding dress. With its square neckline, bands of silver lamé and long sleeves of Nottingham lace, it was the height of fashion.

Left

Green Beads was painted by William Clarke Wontner in 1914, at a time when the world of ancient Greece was idealized in artistic circles as a golden age with beautiful women full of languor and grace.

Right

Actress Emily Mortimer marries Alessandro Nivola in 2003. Her soft empire-line dress, with its sheer sleeves and pretty row of buttons, looks both elegant and relaxed.

Above

Detail from *Reception at Malmaison*, 1802, by François Flameng. Napoleon chases his wife, the style icon Empress Josephine. She popularized the high-waisted empire-line style, which has its roots in ancient Greece. The clinging muslin dresses were at first regarded as scandalously revealing when worn by the fashionable ladies of France.

Right

Seventies brides often chose relaxed dresses demonstrating nostalgic references to rural life. Hair left hanging loose, soft high-waisted smocks and gowns in Indian cotton and muslin became popular. The ideal form of transport to the church for these brides was a pony and trap. Floppy hats and circlets of flowers replaced tiaras and veils.

Following page left

Liza Minnelli marries Peter Allen in 1967. Her high-necked dress with its beautiful lace detailing on the sleeve is reminiscent of Edwardian dresses. Historical influences from the Victorian and Edwardian era became fashionable in the late 1960s and the 1970s.

Following page right

This romantic 1930s wedding dress in stiffened lace and tulle with its ruffled skirt was designed by the House of Chanel. The egalitarian Gabrielle 'Coco' Chanel endorsed the white wedding dress as a must for every bride, rich or poor.

SUBCULTURE AND CONVENTION

Bridal trends are more like costume than fashion, they run parallel to the catwalk and the street, but rarely meet it, preferring to cherry-pick different elements of dress from history. It is an interesting paradox that while marriage is about planning for the future, brides often rely on fashion styles from the past. But as weddings become more secular, they risk becoming just themed parties. Today the Internet advertises Halloween- and medieval-themed weddings, and the Big Day is increasingly about playing to the expectations of an audience. The ceremony and celebration are becoming more and more like theatre with wedding rehearsals and dancing lessons, so a costume is really quite apt. When comedian Matt Lucas celebrated his partnership with Kevin McGee in 2006, a serious civil ceremony in dark suits was followed by a lavish pantomime-themed reception. Saying his vows dressed as Aladdin would not quite have hit the same note.

Contemporary or informal wedding dresses are acceptable in the West, but are largely viewed as unconventional. However, as more women get married later, and couples increasingly pay for their own wedding, the sartorial boundaries are dictated less by the mother of the bride and the bride is left free to choose. The Cinderella white dress, worn once and then packed away in the attic is a new, and extravagant, phenomenon popularized in the twentieth century. But when could a woman today wear a white strapless ball gown again without looking like a displaced bride? Until the end of the Fifties, bridal fashion mirrored eveningwear trends, and women reused their wedding dresses. In the nineteenth century a newly married woman would go visiting in her wedding dress for a season. Nancy Mitford wrote in *Love in a Cold Climate*, her novel about the 1930s, 'As a bride I would have been expected to wear my wedding dress at our first dinner party.' 1950s wives wore their white strapless wedding dresses for parties, but without the lace over-blouse. Even Queen Victoria recycled the lace from her wedding dress for her coronation robes. Today brides rarely wear their own dress again, although they may buy someone else's online at ebay, or buy a dress from a vintage clothing store.

The Fifties was the first decade when teenage girls refused to dress like their mothers. The daring wanted to be surfer chicks, beatniks and biker girls. Their icons were Marilyn Monroe and sex kitten Brigitte Bardot, who married in pink gingham. Manufacturers and department stores were quick to cash in on the new 'youth' market.

Right

Audrey Hepburn and Fred Astaire dance in the 1957 film *Funny Face*. Her dress is by designer Hubert de Givenchy, with whom she formed a close relationship. He helped her to become a style icon with his clean elegant clothes and she promoted his designs with her gamine beauty.

But when it came to getting married, the very rich still chose lavish couture gowns by Cristóbal Balenciaga, Norman Hartnell or Christian Dior, and everyone else followed with a conventional copy from a bridalwear shop or the dressmaker.

In swinging London, Sixties youth found themselves running the show – the shops, the restaurants and the record labels. 'Of all the strands that weave together to make "the Sixties", the concept of autonomous teenage is perhaps the most important,' wrote Jonathon Green in *All Dressed Up*. It was all about youth. But Mary Quant's mod-inspired pinafore dresses and the space-age suits from Courrèges had little impact on conventional brides, who might have chosen a flat fronted off-white dress with wide long skirts, a fitted empire-line bodice, train and a long veil. Less ornate than the Fifties dresses, it was still a 'gown'. The headgear did change though – with flowery or fur-trimmed bonnets, pillbox hats to hold on veils and little bridal headscarves. The daring few flaunted their pins in minis at their weddings, John Bates designed a bridal catsuit and Yves Saint Laurent a flower-covered bikini. Sheer dresses revealing the underwear and paper wedding dresses probably never made it off the pages of the fashion magazines, but a feminine and fun alternative was a short dress in broderie anglaise or lace.

In Paris in 1968 Balenciaga retired, students ran riot on the streets and Emmanuel Ungaro announced 'Let's Kill Couture'. It was all about free love and the spirit of the revolution. At civil services, couples married in jeans. This might have spelled the death of the white dress. But no. By 1971, over eighty percent of wedding gowns sold in America were reputedly white, and floor length. The need to dress for the audience, and meeting the expectations of family and friends was important then, as it is now. 'The girls really didn't want wedding dresses at all,' explained Monica Hickey – a bridal consultant in the 1970s – in a 1997 article in *The New York Times*, 'but most of them succumbed because Grandmother would cut them out of the will if they didn't.' But for the groovy few, there were medieval kaftans, peasant smocks, embroidered Mexican dresses and filmy vintage tea dresses – all for brides. The Barefoot Bride New York boutique opened in 1972 with muslin and eyelet dresses and hats instead of veils. Hickey continued: 'We did a window at Bergdorf's where the bride was in this Indian embroidery and bare feet, holding sheaves of wheat. We were paying court to the hippies; rich hippies, anyway.'

In 1994 Britain relaxed the civil wedding laws, so that brides could now tie the knot in licensed gardens, stately homes or even a supermarket. The UK had been losing out as increasing numbers of couples married in more exciting locations abroad, where they could realize their wishes for unorthodox weddings unsuitable for a church or registry office. There are ever decreasing numbers of weddings in religious settings in the UK. There are skydiving weddings, scuba diving weddings, hot air balloon weddings and nudist weddings. Handfasting ceremonies at sacred sites are popular with alternative religious groups such as Wiccans or Druids. The ritual centres on tying the couple's clasped hands with a cord or ribbon.

New venues called for new wedding dresses. For the beach there were dresses without trains worn with beaded foot jewellery instead of shoes. For evening weddings, one option was to skip the fuss and fittings, and buy a ready-to-wear evening dress in a soft colour. Manufacturers wised up fast, and designers including Valentino and Christian Lacroix started to offer either bridalwear collections with an eveningwear look, or ready-to-wear evening dresses in bridal colours.

For brides at the beginning of the twentieth century, the options were either status symbol dresses by couturiers such as Worth or the dressmaker. By the end of 2007 the average cost of a wedding dress in the UK, according to the most recent Mintel statistics, was a staggering £900. While the very rich might still commission a haute couture Dior dress, the high street stores came to the rescue of the less well-heeled with supermarket wedding dresses at ASDA for £60 in 2007, strapless white dresses at Marks & Spencer for £150, and a wedding dress by Viktor and Rolf at H&M for just over £200. So let's hear it for the rise of the high-street bride. Or failing that, why not have a nudist wedding and spend what you've saved on the honeymoon?

Right

Designer Karl Lagerfeld takes to the catwalk with one of his models at the Chanel couture show for Autumn/Winter 2006–07 in Paris. His understated bride wears a tunic dress over skinny leg trousers.

Above

Underwater weddings and skydiving weddings are just some of the exotic action wedding packages that are being offered to couples today.

Right

Akemi Kito signs a covenant as her groom Hiroshi Matsuoka looks on during their wedding ceremony inside a chapel made of ice at the 'Igloo village' on Lake Shikaribetsu, Northern Japan, in 2007.

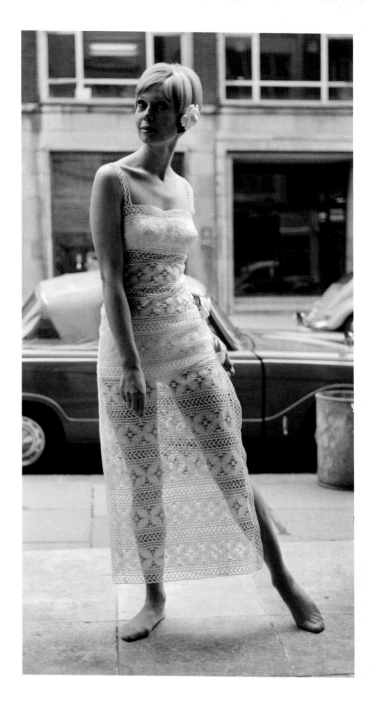

Cilla Black wears a red mini dress on her wedding day in 1969. In the West red is still seen as a daring choice for a bride, as it is the opposite of virginal white, but in China brides wear red because it is seen as an auspicious colour.

Above

Nipa of Hells Angels Finland marries his bride Ursula at a festive ceremony in Uspenski Orthodox Cathedral, Helsinki, in 1999.

Their 1969 marriage ceremony over, Michael Farr and his bride Tracey Austin make their getaway on a motorcycle, leaving behind sixty hippie friends with a wild collection of guitars, flowers and beads. No wedding rings were exchanged, but instead Farr placed chains on a bible to be blessed by the Reverend Ted Noffs.

Right

Mark and Nicola Gamblin, who married in Devon in 2002, drive off after the ceremony dressed in full leathers.

In 1967 Yves Saint Laurent conjured up his bikini bride – model Twiggy wearing a bikini of flowers as a wedding dress. A flower-covered bikini reappeared, here, on the Yves Saint Laurent catwalk for Spring/Summer 1999 in Paris.

Above

Eleven couples bared all for each other on Valentine's Day as they simultaneously exchanged vows at Jamaican holiday resort Hedonism 111 in 2002. Their strategically placed bouquets are vital accessories for the wedding photographs.

Above

Danny McCulloch of British pop group The Animals weds Carol Fielder at Paddington Registry Office in 1967. The bride looks doll-like in her tiny white mini dress.

Right

Dutch Prince Johan Friso and Mabel Wisse Smit leave the City Hall in 2004 in Delft, The Netherlands. The bride's wedding gown was made by Dutch designers Viktor & Rolf, and it took their team of four 600 hours to complete. A grand total of 248 hand-made bows cover the dress and train.

Left

Members of the Rainbow Family, hippies who meet every year at a giant campsite, attend a wedding of a young couple held within a circle of Rainbow Family members in Oregon in 1997.

Above

A young hippie couple marry under the blue sky in 1968 in Los Angeles. The bride wears garlands of flowers in her hair. Unconventional brides at the time married in Egyptian kaftans, embroidered white Mexican dresses or just a pair of jeans.

EAST, WEST, NORTH, SOUTH

As world cultures increasingly bleed into each other, Western weddings can include exciting elements from other cultures, as Anglo-Saxons marry Hindus, and liberal Jews marry West Indians. Some brides yearn to mark their wedding day with a ceremony which steers away from the traditional. Entirely secular ceremonies and weddings on mountains or beaches cannot be ignored, and brides might incorporate customs or venues from cultures that are not their own. It could be a wedding in a riad in Marrakech, or exchanging flower garlands on a Thai beach. From group weddings in China, where one hundred brides make simultaneous vows, to a quickie wedding at Gretna Green or Las Vegas, there are innumerable customs and traditions from which to borrow. Mick Jagger and Jerry Hall married in 1990 in Bali with a Hindu ceremony (see page 198). Kurt Cobain and Courtney Love married on a beach in Hawaii in 1992. Today you can even tie the knot at a Mayan Indian ceremony amongst the ancient ruins in Mexico's Yucatan Peninsula. Or, for the all-American experience, Disneyland offers wedding deals that include a ride in Cinderella's coach.

Sometimes new traditions and new cultural identities are built by blurring the boundaries between religions, customs and continents. In Japan, although traditional weddings are Shinto and held at a shrine, some Japanese brides are introducing white dresses and traditional Western wedding customs. Some weddings are even held in church as secular Christian-style ceremonies. 'Japanese and western bridal fashions are worn, rings are exchanged in a Shinto-style ceremony, French dinner is served for a reception, and a wedding cake is cut by a couple wearing wedding kimonos… the women I interviewed identified their wedding experiences as uniquely Japanese,' wrote Masami Suga in *Wedding Dress Across Cultures*. They are making the ceremony their own, and do not view it as Western at all.

Fashion designers find inspiration from other cultures to come up with new cuts, colours or ornamentation. During the late Sixties and early Seventies designers happily went on the rampage, globetrotting through the continents to dress the flower power generation. Winter brides in the Seventies wore maxi-coats with white mink cuffs, for a glamorous *Doctor Zhivago* look. Different cultures and dress around the globe continue to influence designers including Yves Saint Laurent, John Galliano and Jean-Paul Gaultier.

Right

The Brazilian supermodel Gisele Bundchen attends a gala at the Metropolitan Museum of Art in New York in 2006. Her body-skimming bias-cut dress is detailed at the hem with the fringes and embroidery of a traditional Spanish scarf.

When a bride and groom are from different religions, they may have two religious leaders presiding over their service, perhaps a rabbi and a priest. For a Jain Indian and French-Belgian Christian ceremony in America, the first half took place under a mandap canopy with an Indian priest, and the second half was a traditional Western ceremony. A Chinese and American couple had a Chinese tea ceremony at the end of a Western civil service. The bride can combine elements from both traditions in her dress, or have two wedding outfits. Some Chinese brides wear white Western gowns for the ceremony, and then change into a red cheongsam, a gown with side slits. Couples from different religions and cultures, who can afford it, may decide on two separate ceremonies. American Hindus might have a civil ceremony first, and then the next day a Hindu ceremony with the groom arriving on a white horse. Then there will be a Western-style reception with dinner and dancing on the third day. The bride would need at least three dresses. The ceremonies might be held in two different countries. When actress Elizabeth Hurley married Arun Nayar in 2007 she had, at first, a civil ceremony at Sudeley Castle, England, and then flew to Jodhpur in India for six days of traditional Indian festivities (see pages 186–187). She swapped her vintage-inspired white Versace ball gown for a series of celebration dresses. While the Western papers dubbed her a Bridezilla, India's *Economic Times* was kinder: 'The Elizabeth Hurley–Arun Nayar wedding at Jodhpur gave Indians a first-hand introduction to a concept that's already big in the west – Destination Weddings. Dancing horses, walkways lined with hot red chilli peppers and endless parties against the backdrop of an exotic Rajasthan palace, the wedding had it all.'

As wedding budgets soar, couples in the West can't resist prolonging the party. A Muslim wedding lasts five days, with a series of different ceremonies. A traditional British wedding thirty-five years ago comprised just one evening for the stag or hen party, a marriage on a weekday afternoon and a drinks reception afterwards. Now there are stag weeks abroad, pre-wedding dinners, and often a post-wedding Sunday lunch for all the guests. Festivities are becoming more drawn-out and much more expensive, more like a Muslim or Hindu wedding. So bring on the six-day white wedding feast in the West. And that means six dresses for the bride.

Left

The bride looks on during her wedding ceremony in 2007 in the village of Galicnik in Macedonia. The Galicnik Wedding is a three-day traditional Macedonian wedding celebration, held each Petrovden or St Peter's Day, which blends pagan and Christian customs.

Above

This Pakistani bride sits during a mass wedding ceremony of over fifty couples in Lahore in 2006. Marriage is expensive and some parents turn to the idea of mass marriages where many couples tie the knot simultaneously, which helps to spread the cost.

HELLO!

No. 960 • 13 MARCH 2007 • £1.90

WORLD EXCLUSIVE

JOIN US INSIDE SUDELEY CASTLE FOR

ELIZABETH AND ARUN'S

LAVISH ENGLISH WEDDING

HELLO!

NUMBER 961 • 20 MARCH 2007 • £1.90

WORLD EXCLUSIVE

ELIZABETH AND ARUN'S MAGNIFICENT HINDU WEDDING IN INDIA

53-PAGE ALBUM
- NON-STOP FESTIVITIES
- PALACE CRICKET MATCH
- BOLLYWOOD DANCING
- SACRED CEREMONY
- SPECTACULAR FIREWORKS

Jordanian grooms and brides take
part in a mass wedding ceremony in
Amman in 2007. A Jordanian Islamic
charity organized a mass wedding
for thirty-two couples to help young
people unable to afford expensive
ceremonies.

Previous left

When actress Elizabeth Hurley
married Arun Nayar in 2007 she wore
a white vintage-inspired Versace ball
gown for the civil ceremony
at Sudeley Castle, England.

Right

A model walks the catwalk at the
Alexander McQueen Spring/Summer
2007 show in Paris. His play on the
traditional Spanish mantilla veil,
which is usually held up high on the
head with a comb, is here supported
by flowers and wrapped around the
body to form a body-skimming cloak
of lace.

Previous right

Elizabeth Hurley dresses as an Indian
bride at her wedding to Arun Nayar,
wearing a hot pink couture sari by
Versace. The couple tied the knot in
a traditional six-day Hindu wedding
ceremony in 2007 in Jodhpur, India.

Left

Socialite Jemima Goldsmith marries Pakistani cricket star Imran Khan at a civil service in Richmond, London, in 1995. She converted to Islam, and they also had a short Islamic ceremony in Paris. She wears a cream bias-cut silk skirt and jacket by Bruce Oldfield.

Above

Jordan's King Hussein stands with new bride American Lisa Halaby at the royal palace in 1978. She also converted to Islam before the marriage and changed her name to Noor. For the wedding she wore a simple long white crepe dress with bell sleeves by Dior.

Above

Crown Prince Hamzah of Jordan and his bride Princess Noor walk arm-in-arm at their wedding celebrations in 2004 in Amman, Jordan. Hamzeh and Noor registered their marriage in 2003.

Right

A couple leaves after reporting their marriage to a statue of former North Korean leader Kim Il Sung in 2002 in Pyongyang, North Korea. Traditional bridal dress is a chogori, a jacket tied around the body with ribbons, and a chima, a full-length wraparound skirt. A white sash and a headpiece decorated with flowers and tiny pendants complete the look.

Left

An Indian model shows off a wedding outfit by fashion designer Bharat Singer during a fashion show in the Indian city of Ahmedabad in 2006. The fiery opulence makes a Western white wedding dress seem dull in comparison.

Above

Diamonds sparkled and cannons boomed when the daughter of one of the world's richest reigning monarchs Princess Majeedah Nuurul Bulqiah married Pengiran Khairul Khalil. Here they sit together at the start of their traditional wedding ceremony at the Nurul Iman Palace in Brunei in 2007. She holds a bouquet of diamond-studded flowers.

Left

A model walks the runway during Japanese designer Yumi Katsura's wedding dress fashion show in 2006 in Sichuan Province, China.

Above

His Imperial Highness Prince Akishino of Japan (known as Prince Aya) and his new wife, Princess Akishino Kiko, marry wearing traditional Japanese wedding clothes in 1990 in Tokyo.

Model Jerry Hall marries Rolling Stone Mick Jagger in Bali in 1990. She wears traditional Balinese costume.

Above

The Chinese empress Wan Jung is pictured here during her marriage with Pu-Yi, in 1922. She was a renowned beauty, and her seventeen-year-old husband is known as the last emperor of China. He chose her from a photograph.

Above

Film star Loretta Young plays an heiress in the 1937 film *Café Metropole*. She wears a hooded lace cloak, which could double up as coat and veil.

Right

Bride Tazuko Kojima wears a traditional Japanese wedding dress in 1989 in Kyoto, Japan. The white head covering is to hide the 'horns of jealousy', symbolizing that she will become a gentle, obedient wife.

Actress Elizabeth Hurley wears a
dress by Dior at the Victoria & Albert
Museum in 2007 in London.
The asymmetric bodice, designed
by John Galliano, is reminiscent
of an Indian sari.

Above

Pop singer and actor Adam Faith
marries dancer Jackie Irving at Caxton
Hall registry office in London in 1967.
Many Sixties and Seventies designers
used djellabahs as inspiration for coats
and dresses at the time.

RITUAL

Traditionally a wedding is a rite of passage where a woman gives up her primary role as her father's daughter to become her husband's wife. It symbolizes the right to bear children and the transition from virgin to woman. In the past it has been an important ritual for women, often bringing status and commanding respect within a community. Historically, in many cultures marriage was a financial arrangement between two families. Today in the West it is usually a love match between two individuals who may not be virgins. Matrimonial customs, made popular before women's equality, often subjugate a bride to anachronistic stereotypes – virgin and chattel. Old traditions are still being used at weddings, but often in a changed form, while other rituals have been phased out as outdated. Then there are new developments – multiple best men, women giving speeches and more Asian brides adopting the Western white dress. Marriage rituals are in a constant state of flux.

Betrothal is about sealing the deal and is steeped in materialistic tradition. The diamond engagement ring is derived from the practice of buying a bride, as betrothal was often marked by a financial contract between two families. There is still the view that an engagement ring should cost the bridegroom one to two months of his salary today. In medieval times, the bounty with which the groom purchased the hand of his betrothed included precious stones. A ring was also seen as an object that a bride could sell if she was widowed.

In many cultures, the couple's families exchanged money or goods. In the West today, the bride's family traditionally pays for the wedding. In Europe, until Victorian times, the bride's family would give a dowry of money, goods or valuables to the family of the groom. And in return the groom paid a price for the bride and promised to support her. In Africa, before a marriage is agreed, the groom offers a 'bride price' of money and goods such as goats, cattle and cowrie shells. Today many Hindus and certain African societies still adhere to the dowry tradition, even though this practice has been banned in some places. In India, in extreme cases, it can result in horrors such as female infanticide by parents who cannot afford the dowry for a girl, and bride burning if a groom's family feels his wife's dowry is too meagre.

Right

In 1972 María del Carmen Martínez-Bordiú y Franco, granddaughter of General Franco, marries Don Alfonso, Duke of Anjou and Cádiz, grandson of King Alfonso XIII of Spain. General Franco is on the far left. The wedding took place in the chapel of the Palacio del Prado.

Left

A bride and groom float in a tidal pool in Bermuda. As wedding ceremonies become more secular there is an ever-increasing demand for weddings in exciting and original locations.

A bride was often expected to enter into marriage spiritually and physically pure: as a virgin, and cleansed in body and mind. Ritual purification is still an important preparation for marriage. In London, a girl might visit a beauty salon while a traditional Jewish bride will fully immerse herself in a mikveh bath, and Indian Muslim women have turmeric spread all over their bodies before they bathe. More extreme are women from the Gewi in Botswana, who fast for four days in complete silence, and then have their hair shaved off by the village elders before their big day. Most disturbing is the fading custom of female circumcision as a rite of passage to adulthood, which makes a women eligible for marriage in parts of southern Africa. Veiling was often seen as protecting a bride from the evil eye, as well as a symbol of virginity. Indian and Pakistani brides have henna patterns painted on their hands and feet, as if to veil the whole body. At a Christian wedding the groom lifts the veil; whereas a Jewish groom places the veil over his wife's face, to show he will clothe and protect her.

Clothing can mark the exchange. A Hindu bride will arrive in clothes bought by her parents, and then leave in a sari bought by her husband, showing the transition of financial responsibility. In parts of Somalia, a bride's teeth may be filed, a beauty ritual which is often paid for by the groom. In Japan, a bride ritually changes her clothes up to five times. Her white kimono symbolizes death in her parents' home, and rebirth in her husband's, and the new coloured clothes signify acceptance into the groom's family. Equally, there are rituals of exchange between the bride and groom. Hindus exchange garlands of flowers. During Christian, Russian Orthodox and many civil ceremonies today, the bride and groom exchange wedding rings. The Romans exchanged iron bands to symbolize binding the marriage – and also the man's ownership over his wife.

Some closing rituals at the end of a ceremony are acts of remembrance that honour the past. African-Americans sometimes jump over a broom, as this was the symbolic act of marriage for slave communities who were forbidden legal weddings. At a Jewish ceremony, the groom stamps on a glass as a reminder of the destruction of the Temples. Others are symbols of fertility, such as the old tradition of throwing wheat at the bride and groom. In the Middle Ages the wedding guests threw small sweet cakes instead, which pre-empted the large wedding cake of today.

Muslims shower the bride with coins; Mexicans throw red beads. And releasing live butterflies instead of throwing rice or confetti is today's latest trend.

A bride was expected to lose her virginity on her wedding night, and matrimonial traditions celebrate this transition, often heckling the bride and groom before they retire to bed. Tossing the bouquet is an English tradition; when guests tried to rip a piece of the bride's dress or flowers as a keepsake, the bride threw a bouquet to distract them. In France they threw a garter. Few cultures now exhibit the bloodied sheet the next morning to prove virginity and consummation. A bride living on the Marquesas Islands in Polynesia was historically required to have sex with all the male guests at her wedding, saving the groom for last. Fortunately this is now an outdated tradition.

Arranged marriages are numerous in the Middle East and parts of Africa and Asia, but now in countries such as Japan it is tackled more like internet dating. There is, however, a darker side to arranged marriages. Illegal child marriages in Egypt, Afghanistan, Bangladesh, Ethiopia, Pakistan, India and the Middle East might take place in rural communities, where young children can be married off aged eleven or younger. Worse is today's violent tradition of bride kidnapping still common in several Central Asian countries. The groom and his family abduct a woman as a potential bride. There is a social stigma about saying no, and the family can hold her hostage for days. Although illegal in Kyrgyzstan, kidnappers are rarely prosecuted. In Ethiopia and Rwanda women can be kidnapped and raped, with the intention of making them pregnant so that no one else will marry them. The word honeymoon is thought to have its origins in bridal kidnap, symbolizing the month that a man went into hiding in the hope of making his 'bride' pregnant within one lunar cycle. This is certainly one wedding tradition we could do without.

Left

The groom slips a wedding ring onto his bride's finger at a 1950s wedding. During Christian, Russian Orthodox, Jewish and many other civil ceremonies today, the bride and groom exchange wedding rings.

Above

A ring is placed on a bride's finger at a Hindu wedding in 1997. A Hindu bride will usually wear gold wedding jewellery including a mangalsutra necklace of black beads and gold, a thaali necklace with a gold pendant at the centre, a bichhua toe ring and a set of bangles.

Hadas Hanun and Joseph Hanoun marry in the Jewish community of Neve Dekalim, Gaza Strip, Israel, in 2005. They stand underneath a huppah, or traditional Jewish wedding canopy.

Right

Queen Elizabeth and the Duke of Edinburgh receive a blessing from the Archbishop of Canterbury Lord Fisher at their wedding in London in 1947. Norman Hartnell designed her dress, and her long tulle veil was held in place by a diamond tiara.

Left

Brazilian model Isabeli Fontana marries actor Henri Castelli in an evening ceremony on the beach in Rio de Janeiro, Brazil, in 2005. Their 700 guests, at the couple's request, all wore white. Here her father gives her away. Her dress has an open back with a bikini fastening and she wears foot jewellery rather than sandals.

Above

Zinzi Mandela marries in Johannesburg, South Africa, in 1992. She is shown here with her father, Nelson Mandela.

Left

Elsie Gosling and her new husband, who is president of the mixed tandem bike club Solon, walk under a triumphal arch made of bicycles held up by their club members after their London wedding in 1936.

Above

A bride and groom step through a six-foot ring covered in pansies at their wedding ceremony in California in 1947. The bridesmaids' circular headdresses echo the round pansy ring. They wear veils and carry bouquets to match the bride.

This mass wedding procession of 122 couples, mainly members of the armed services, were given grants by the Nazi authorities to enable them to marry in 1938.

Middle left

A wedding procession lines up at a mass wedding in Jamaica in 1950.

Bottom left

A wedding procession walks through the French village of Mont-près-Chambord in December 1948.

Right

Prince Juan Carlos of Spain and Princess Sophia of Greece pose with their guests on the steps of the royal palace in Athens, after their wedding ceremony in 1962.

Above

Russian Olga Rostropovich marries
Olaf Guerrand-Hermes in a grand
1991 ceremony officiated by French
President Jacques Chirac in Paris.

Right

Napoleon I marries Marie Louise
of Habsburg-Lorraine in 1810. For
her official church wedding she wore
a white muslin Regency column dress.

VIRGIN, SIREN, MOTHER, WIFE

Western women have it all. They can take the Pill, have sex, bag a husband and still walk down the aisle on their father's arm in a white dress. Then they can get divorced and marry someone else. Virgin? Siren? Mother? Wife? Cohabiting girlfriend? Divorcee? Widow? A woman can experience many of these roles before her thirties, and in different orders. She may be a pregnant bride, a lesbian bride, a lesbian pregnant bride, or have her own children there at the ceremony. There are enormous differences between a teenage Asian bride at her arranged marriage and a Western woman in her thirties marrying the man with whom she has lived for four years.

In the West, the ritual of marriage does not often signify the transition of virgin to wife to mother. So does the white dress, which suggests purity and virginity, have any relevance at all? The average age for UK marriages in 1975 was reputedly nineteen; in 2007 the most recent Mintel research calculated it at twenty-eight. Western women now have power and choices that were once undreamt of. They are often older as brides, and can choose to disregard the virginal princess bride stereotype. But there may be a difference between what a bride wants to wear, and what she is expected to wear. As weddings today in the West are often less about the joining of families, the community expectation of, say, a white dress, is sometimes disregarded for the individual's wishes. And yet in spite of a woman's independence, the wedding day is one of the only times that she might admit to dressing for an audience, and her man. The bridal industry encourages this with tips on how to choose the perfect dress to look beautiful for the groom. Brides sometimes choose dresses which differ enormously from their day-to-day style. This may result from the pressure that she feels – she must appear to be the most beautiful bride when the groom first sets eyes on her at the ceremony.

A traditional white wedding is not always what a bride wants for a second, third or fourth wedding. In the 1970s it became easier to get a divorce, and this led to the rise of the second wedding. There are loose guidelines of what is socially acceptable – a shorter veil that does not cover the face, or replacing the veil with a hat or flowers. American journalist Helen Rowland quipped: 'A bride at her second marriage does not wear a veil. She wants to see what she is getting.' Dresses are not expected to be full length, and

Right

American divorcee Mrs Wallis Simpson marries the Duke of Windsor in France in 1937. He had already abdicated as King Edward VIII of England in order to take her as his bride. Paris couturier Mainbocher made her blue crepe wedding dress, and soon afterwards fashionable ladies began to order clothes in 'Wallis blue'.

can be off-white or not white at all. But equally, a white dress is
perfectly acceptable at a second wedding, and quite rightly so
if a bride feels comfortable in one. There are no rules. It may be
a chance for a woman to show her sense of individuality, how
she has moved on from acting out a role as the first-time fairytale
bride; that this time around it is more real, and more about her
choices. It is a fantastic chance to buy a beautiful evening dress
or suit that can be worn again, a grown-up choice, rather than
the once-in-a-lifetime dream.

Coco Chanel cruelly remarked, 'There is no fashion for the old.'
But there is a big difference between the dress that a fifty-five-year-
old and a twenty-year-old bride would choose. Elegant femininity
over a slinky bias-cut dress is probably the way to go, with a hat
or headpiece rather than a veil. Neat tailoring, or a long but not
full-length dress, may be more flattering. There are wraps for the
winter, and boleros and thin jackets for the summer as cover-ups
for the arms and neck. Camilla Parker Bowles pitched it perfectly at
her 2005 marriage to Prince Charles (see page 238) – sophisticated
but suitably correct, and nothing like his first wife. While it has
been important for brides in the past to appear virginal and
demure, some modern women today want to look sexy on their
wedding day too. The strapless gown means that even traditional
brides now show their shoulders and arms, as they never would
have done before. Oscar de la Renta is not sure about this. He
was quoted saying: 'Lately, there has been a lot of skin exposed in
wedding dresses. I'm from a Catholic country, so it's always a little
bit difficult [for me], this idea of walking half-naked into a church.'
But designers such as Badgley Mischka and Collette Dinnigan
are making some seriously sexy dresses for brides. After all, if
you're not a virgin, do you really need to look demure on your
wedding day?

When the UK Civil Partnership Act was passed in 2004, providing
same-sex couples the same rights under civil marriage as straight
couples, a new 'gay wedding' industry quickly sprung up.
The original government projection that there would be 20,000
married gays by 2010 had been reached by 2007. But what do two
brides at a wedding wear? Some choose two traditional bridal
gowns or two evening dresses. For other couples, one might opt
for a white dress while the other goes for a neat trouser or skirt
suit. There are no rules.

Above

Actress Elizabeth Taylor is photographed in a limousine in 1950 in Beverly Hills with her new husband Conrad 'Nicky' Hilton, Jr. MGM studio designer Helen Rose made her white satin ball gown. Her pearl tiara complemented the seed pearl detailing on the dress and she carried a bouquet of white orchids. Taylor was married eight times to seven husbands.

Right

Mattel launched this Elizabeth Taylor doll (bottom right) as part of its Timeless Treasures celebrity line. It shows Taylor in her bridal costume from the film *Father of the Bride*. The movie star married Eddie Fisher in Las Vegas in 1959 (bottom left), Richard Burton for the first time in 1964 (top right) and Michael Wilding in 1952 (top left) wearing an elegant New Look-style suit.

Left

Space Age bride. Supermodel Kate Moss models a *Star Trek*-style wedding dress for Versace in 1995. The all-silver-and-white collection took its influences from Sixties minimalism with stiff mini dresses and zip fastenings. This dress may be unlikely to turn up at an altar, but at least it is a world away from Victorian-style ballgowns.

Above

Anthony Ruivivar as Carlos and Yvonne Jung as Holly star in a 2005 episode of *Third Watch*. The two actors are married. Jung's slinky dress demonstrates how a gown that reveals the arms and shoulders no longer looks unsuitable for a wedding day.

Socialites Mr and Mrs Russell Firestone
Jnr talk to a little girl on a tricycle
after their wedding at Riverside
Church, New York, in 1965. Her neat
white suit and simple take on the veil
would suit a bride at a second wedding
today who wanted a more low-key
sartorial approach.

Right

Suited and booted. American actress
Jennifer O'Neill walks with her
husband Joseph Koster after their
wedding ceremony in New York in
the 1970s, wearing a simple skirt suit.
She married and divorced nine times.

Camilla, Duchess of Cornwall, pulls it off in a sartorial triumph at her marriage to Prince Charles in England in 2005. She looks stylishly dressed for someone of her age and station. Philip Treacy designed her magnificent headpiece with its gold-leafed feathers tipped with Swarovski crystals, and her long blue silk dress and coat were by Robinson Valentine. This was her second marriage.

Above

Countess Spencer marries Jean-François de Chambrun in 1993, aged sixty-three. She was stepmother to Diana, Princess of Wales. Her flower-print dress is by Emmanuel Ungaro, a daring choice for an older bride; but with the deep pink veiled headdress the overall result is vibrant and fun, albeit a little eccentric.

Left

Lesbian wedding. What do two brides wear on their wedding day? If the brides are not opting for a trouser suit and a dress, two white long 'goddess' dresses offers a stylish solution.

Right

Comedian Matt Lucas and Kevin McGee tied the knot at a civil service in suits in 2006. For their reception, at Banqueting House in London, however, they went for full fancy dress as Aladdin and Prince Charming.

Previous left

In 1951 American pop singer Frank Sinatra poses with his wife, the movie star and sex symbol Ava Gardner, on their wedding day.

Previous right

Actress and beauty Felicia Farr kisses her new husband Jack Lemmon in 1962 after their wedding ceremony in Paris. Her V-neck, sleeveless lace dress is perfectly understated, as is the veil which sits lightly over her face and hair like a carefully spun cobweb.

Above

Widow and bride. Mrs Jean Gibbs, widow of Captain Vicary Gibbs, marries Captain Andrew Elphinstone, a nephew of the Queen. The bride was lady-in-waiting to Princess Elizabeth.

Right

Wallis Warfield, stylish with her unusual divided veil, poses for the camera in her wedding dress in 1916. This was her first marriage. Her third was to Prince Edward, Duke of Windsor.

Left

Popstar Kylie Minogue plays to the camera at the John Galliano Autumn/ Winter 2007–08 collection during Paris Fashion Week. A bride who wants to avoid a floor-length ball gown could try a neat little strapless white dress similar to this one. The detailing at the neckline helps to enhance the bust.

Right

Davinia Taylor wears a floor-length dress by designer Ben De Lisi in 2004. It was made from satin-backed crepe and covered with 300 pearls. This dress was designed for the BAFTAs, but would work just as well for a bride today craving the glamour of the red carpet.

Zsa Zsa Gabor, the Hungarian actress and socialite, married nine times. Her first husband was Burhan Belge, whom she married in 1937 (bottom left). She married George Sanders (opposite) in Las Vegas, in 1949. Her fourth marriage was to Herbert Hutner (bottom right) in New York in 1962, and in 1966 she married her fifth husband, Joshua Cosden (top right). Her sixth husband was former actor Jack Ryan (top left). They married at Caesar's Palace, Las Vegas in 1975, but divorced the following year.

Bikini bride. Baywatch star Pamela Anderson ties the knot demurely in 2006 with Kid Rock on a yacht in St Tropez. The bride reputedly changed three times: out of a pink bikini and hot pants, into a tiara, veil and white lace dress, then into this white bikini. In 2007 she married Rick Salomon wearing a cream denim mini dress by Valentino.

Right

Actress Terri J. Vaughn plays the bride in *All Of Us* in 2004. Her sexy dress, with its lace-up detailing is set off perfectly by a cool set of minimalist pearls.

COLOUR

When popstar Gwen Stefani strode out like a blushing bride in her pink-tipped wedding dress, it seemed so much more appropriate and pretty than a pure white dress. Although virginity is no longer a pre-requisite for a suitable wife, white is still the most traditional colour for a wedding dress at a Christian or Jewish ceremony today. 'Married in white, you have chosen right,' advises the bossy old English wedding ditty. White is the blank canvas, the colour of angels. White is the combination of all the colours of the spectrum. It is bright, eye-catching and ideal for bride who wants to stand out as the star of the show.

A dash of colour or coloured shoes can liven up a white wedding dress. Leading US bridal retailer David's Bridal offered white gowns in 2007 with coloured embroidery, trims, ribbons or sashes. During the Sixties and Seventies, coloured linings on wedding dresses provided a tantalising flash of pink and lime green. In the Eighties, designer David Fielden used coloured silk flowers emblazoned on white dresses, while Yves Saint Laurent shocked with his dark aubergine wedding dress, which looked black. In 2005 burlesque artist Dita von Teese, bride of Marilyn Manson, wore a dark purple full-skirted wedding gown by Vivienne Westwood (see page 261). The colour alone gave it a deep sophistication that would have been lost in white.

With the increase in secular ceremonies, cross-cultural weddings and second marriages, a virginal white dress can seem inappropriate. For an evening party after a civil service a bride might prefer to whip off her jacket to reveal a slinky coloured evening dress in navy blue. Or she might choose a slip with a swirling Pucci print. At least she can wear it again after the wedding. And why pretend to be a demure virgin if everybody knows you're not? An evening or a bridesmaid's dress in a colour other than white can be an excellent choice.

In the West today, white is understood to stand for virginity, purity and the unsullied maid. But white is also associated with death. It is a Hindu funereal colour, and Victorians in mourning in the colonies wore white dresses with matching weeping veils. In ancient Greece brides wore white as a symbol of joy and purity, and white was worn at some weddings in the Middle Ages as a sign of virginity. The influential Queen Victoria broke royal tradition to marry in

Left

A trio of performers stand with Indian model Sudipa as she poses in a lotus-shaped palanquin in Ahmedabad, India, in 2006. She wears a vibrantly coloured lehenga choli. Indian brides also marry in saris and salwar kameez.

white rather than silver in 1840, sanctioning the white wedding dress as the fashionable choice for brides who could afford it. She then threw the whole country into mourning black when her husband died.

It was not until the 1920s that the forward-thinking Coco Chanel endorsed the white wedding dress as the essential for every bride, rich or poor. It was Chanel who said, 'I care more about the city street than the drawing room.' Once, the lady's maid would never have dreamt of marrying in an extravagant white dress like her mistress. In the nineteenth century she would have probably married in grey or even black. The Twenties democratized dress, thanks to designers Coco Chanel and Jean Patou, as the fashion for clean boyish dresses used minimal fabric and did not have to be over-embellished.

Until the early twentieth century it was perfectly acceptable to get married in pink, blue or just your Sunday best – colour never hinted that a woman's virginity was not intact. Historically blue has affiliations with purity. The ancient Israelites trimmed their wedding clothes with blue ribbons to signify purity, love and fidelity, and Western brides are told to include 'something blue' in their wedding clothes today. Divorcee Wallis Simpson wore an elegant blue-grey Mainbocher wedding dress with a blue and pink headpiece when she scandalously married the abdicating King Edward VIII in 1937 (see page 227). It was copied almost overnight.

If white was a status symbol in the Twenties, it was the opposite at medieval weddings when Western princess brides indulged in the most expensive dyed cloth – red, purple and black – as a show of prosperity. They wore vast dresses in velvet, damask, silk, satin and fur. The fabric dripped with heavy diamonds, rubies and gold thread. It was flashy for a reason. Royal marriages were matches between countries and, at a wedding, a bride flaunted her country's riches. Today Asian Muslim brides choose sparkling, bright clothes – either the heavily-embroidered, colourful lehenga (an elegant long skirt and blouse) or the salwar kameez (a long blouse over trousers). They adorn their bodies with jewellery, flowers and henna tattoos. In Japan, an upper-class bride at a Shinto ceremony changes out of the white swinging-sleeved wedding kimono – the shiromuku – into a brightly coloured wedding kimono, then into a Western-style white wedding dress, and finally into a coloured evening gown for the reception. She may also even add a full-sleeved kimono, a furisode.

Colour could also be an indicator of social class. White was often associated with the upper classes as it dirties easily, and was therefore expensive to look after. In Korea, during the Chosun Dynasty, queens wore red or yellow wonsam ceremonial robes as brides, upper-class women and princesses wore green with gold leaf, and everyone else was only allowed to wear plain green for weddings and funerals.

'Married in red, you'll wish yourself dead,' goes the rhyme, and by the Victorian era in the West, red had associations with scarlet women. In the East the connotations are very different. The Chinese see red as lucky, a symbol of strength, happiness and permanence, and a colour that keeps evil spirits away. Today Chinese brides wear red dresses, adorned with gold and silver designs, although some brides prefer a Western-style white dress instead. Traditional Hindu weddings are far from sombre affairs, with the bride in a deep red sari flecked with gold, surrounded by handfuls of bright flowers. In Northern India the traditional colour of women's wedding garments is red, or green for fertility. In South India women often now get married in white or cream. In the West, wearing green used to be seen as the fairies' colour, which risks attracting bad luck.

For many, wearing black as a bride is the ultimate taboo, as it is a symbol of mourning in the West. That didn't stop Oscar de la Renta designing a beautiful black wedding dress. But Holly Brubach did have a point in *A Dedicated Follower of Fashion* when she wrote, 'If weddings reflected all the ambiguities of married life, the bride would wear gray.'

A model wears a black wedding dress with a veil during the Oscar de la Renta fashion show for Spring/Summer 1999. A black wedding dress can look sexy and alluring, particularly for an evening reception after a ceremony, but the funereal overtones stop many brides from making what is still such a daring sartorial statement. However, a black trim, sash, or black embroidery on a white dress looks stylish while being less obviously provocative.

Burlesque star Dita von Teese certainly knew how to make a statement at her wedding to Marilyn Manson in 2005. Her Vivienne Westwood gown was bright violet and made out of seventeen metres of Swiss silk. Her hat was by milliner Stephen Jones and her shoes by Christian Louboutin.

Above

Something blue. Actress Debbie Reynolds and husband Harry Karl tie the knot. In the West, blue symbolizes purity and has at times been regarded as a purer colour than white.

Right

Movie star Elizabeth Taylor marries Richard Burton in 1964. Her pale ochre wedding empire-line dress and headdress of fresh flowers make Taylor look relaxed and natural. In ancient Rome, brides wore long white dresses with a veil of flame yellow called the flammeum, and sometimes wore yellow shoes to match.

Left

Audrey Hepburn poses with her new husband psychiatrist Dr Andrea Dotti after their 1969 wedding. Her pale pink mini dress is reminiscent of the 1960s Space-Age angular designs by André Courrèges. Bonnets and headscarves were a fashionable alternative to the veil.

Previous left

Movie star Gwyneth Paltrow is photographed in Los Angeles in 2007. She looks classy and glamorous in this capped sleeve Zac Posen dress with a train. A bride opting for an evening reception may want to consider a colour other than white.

Above

A groom bicycles through Paris with his bride. In the early twentieth century a once-worn white wedding dress was still the preserve of the rich. Everyone else married in their Sunday best which was often grey or black.

Previous right

Actress Liv Tyler walks to her wedding reception with her husband Royston Langdon in New York in 2003. Her gold empire-line waistband and pink shoes add a dash of fun to the soft romantic white dress, and the shoes even pick up the colour of the groom's tie.

American model Zofia Borucka marries actor Jean Reno in Les Baux de Provence, France, in 2006. Her pale yellow dress adds warmth to her tanned skin, and looks feminine against the starkness of his all-white suit. The dress is reminiscent of the designs of early-twentieth-century designer Madeleine Vionnet.

Right

Kerry Washington arrives at a Cannes film screening in 2007. She accessorized her tulle dress by Jean Paul Gaultier couture with a Bulgari necklace and a Swarovski clutch bag. This feminine dress would suit a bride with taste for romance, but one who wanted to steer away from the obvious white.

English rose. Movie star and beauty Keira Knightley arrives at the premiere of *Atonement* in 2007. Her feminine strapless dress, with its pink sash, is typical of the relaxed dresses that some brides wear today at summer weddings. A coloured sash is a modern and easy way to break up an all-white dress.

Above

Actress Romy Schneider marries Daniel Biasini in 1975 in Berlin. She wears a floral empire-line dress with wide sleeves tiered with frills. The circlet of flowers pulled over her curls gives her a cherubic look. Her printed dress is loose and flowing, a look which became very popular at the time for its contrast to the geometric mini dresses of the Sixties.

After a three-day wedding celebration, Bollywood stars Abhishek Bachchan and Aishwarya Rai touch a golden statue during a temple visit in India. He wears white kurta pyjamas and Rai dresses in an opulent red sari.

Above

Elaborate local headdresses and embroidered jackets make a dramatic impression at this typical Muslim wedding in Banda Aceh, Indonesia. Tradition dictates that the bride and groom dress with similar attention to detail.

IT'S ALL IN THE DETAIL

As with all codes of dress, detail and accessories can make or break a bride's look. The right underwear can revolutionize the posture and figure, just as the wrong veil can massacre an elegant dress. Wedding fads from lace skull caps to wax flowers come and go, but crucially the accessories need to enhance the dress, and of course the woman inside it. According to tradition, the Western bride should wear something old, something new, something borrowed and something blue. Collectively, they are supposed to bring continuity and tradition, hope and new beginnings, support from friends, and fidelity. Something old could be a vintage dress, or a piece of family lace for a veil, while something blue is a great excuse to introduce some colour to a white dress – blue shoes, a blue sash or a neat row of blue buttons inching down the spine. Or how about a high-kitsch baby blue veil and matching garter?

'Harriet looked modest for the first time in her life in a long French lace veil,' claimed Elizabeth Fremantle (née Wynne) in *The Journals of Elizabeth Fremantle* in the 1950s. Veils are a crucial part of conservative bridal dress. In the West they are usually white, in China they are red, and in ancient Roman times they were golden and would also be used as the burial shroud. They were thought to fend off mischievous evil spirits, and at early arranged marriages they helped to shield the bride from her future husband's curious gaze. A veil mimics long, flowing hair and is often viewed as a symbol of virginity.

So how does a bride even start to choose the right veil? The two main decisions to make are the length and the style. As a guide, it's the shorter the dress, the longer the veil. A cheeky fly-away short veil will show off the back of dress, a grand cathedral veil will drag behind the dress on a train for full drama. Then it's the style. Mantilla? Birdcage? Blusher? Tulle or lace are usual, but more interesting was the Armani Privé silk veil which matched the dress, shown at the Paris couture shows in 2007. And if wearing a virginal veil seems like an anachronism, then lose the veil. It only really came back into fashion in about 1860, and throughout the twentieth century women have chosen straw summer hats, feathers and bonnets over veils. Arguably the most stylish was Bianca Jagger's wide-brimmed hat with its gauzy veil in St Tropez at her 1971 Rolling Stone wedding.

Right

Brazilian top model Isabeli Fontana marries actor Henri Castelli in an evening ceremony on the beach in 2005 in Rio de Janeiro, Brazil. Her unconventional silk muslin mini dress by Versace, with its short skirt and long ruffled train, sported a daring bikini-style back. Swarovski crystals pin-pricking the bodice provided a touch of beach glamour, and a circlet of white flowers on the bride's long hair looked natural and unpretentious for a beach wedding.

Left

With batteries of cameramen and hundreds of celebrity-seekers on hand for the wedding, Pasquale 'Pat' DiCicco, actor's agent, and his bride, Gloria Vanderbilt, leave the historical Santa Barbara Mission where they were married in 1941. The bride was seventeen years old.

Once the veil is decided, then what will attach it to the head? Flowers or diamonds? Lace or pearls? Or just a hidden hairgrip? The most romantic is a traditional wreath of flowers or herbs. Historically rosemary and myrtle, a symbol of fertility, were the most popular. But where country girls chose wild flowers or gilded leaves and wheat, the royals and nobles held their heads high in tiaras and crown jewels. As a bride in 1840, Queen Victoria charmingly wore a crown of orange blossom instead of royal diamonds and set a trend. From 1900 to the 1920s brides wore tiaras of diamonds, diamanté and wired-up lace or even turbans. At Eastern Orthodox weddings the bride and groom both wear traditional crowns, but at a Christian or Jewish ceremony a tiara today is purely a fashion choice. In Korea, a delicate crown decorated with beading, flowers and tiny pendants is part of the bridal dress. Modern tiaras are ethereal wire concoctions threaded with pearls and semi-precious stones – think Queen Titania rather than Princess Diana.

With a white dress, jewellery looks most effective when it is kept simple, be it one showpiece necklace, a pair of glinting diamond earrings or a fairytale tiara. Diamonds and pearls are traditional for brides. Queen Elizabeth II's wedding dress, designed by Norman Hartnell, included 10,000 seed pearls in the ornate embroidery. Crystals, beads and pearls can look beautiful when they are scattered over the fabric of a dress rather than worn on the skin, so that the bride glimmers as she glides down the aisle. At her 2001 wedding Jennifer Lopez went for high-octane glamour in a Valentino wedding dress with sheer sleeves peppered with sparkling stones. And the new trend for black or coloured beads on a bodice can take away the need for jewellery altogether.

Garlands of flowers look natural, feminine and informal. They make perfect accessories for a summer wedding. Flowers have always been used at marriages, be it orange blossom garlanded round the skirts of a Victorian wedding dress, one perfect rose attached to the veil of a Sixties bride, a neat wartime corsage or a vast 1920s shower bouquet trailing yards of ribbon love knots. Orange blossom was prized as a symbol of fertility, as it both blooms and bears fruit at the same time. Most Western brides carry a bouquet or posy, which once would have contained herbs that were consumed at the wedding feast.

'I have spread my dreams under your feet; Tread softly because you tread on my dreams,' wrote W. B. Yeats in his poem *Cloths of Heaven*.

Shoes are barely visible at a wedding, but crucially they add height, and sometimes a flash of colour. Actress Liv Tyler wore a pretty pair of pink shoes which were just visible peeping out from under her white wedding dress (see page 265). Anglo-Saxon brides tossed shoes rather than bouquets to bridesmaids who hoped to be the next to marry, and shoes are still tied to the back of the newlyweds' car to bring good luck. Contemporary bridal shoes range from strappy stilettos by designers Manolo Blahnik and Jimmy Choo, to Christian Louboutin's special order blue-soled bridal range. For beach, informal and summer weddings, easier shoes are beaded flat sandals or pretty flip flops with flat or with wedge heels.

It takes time and preparation to transform the girl-next-door into a blushing bride, with flawless skin and natural make-up. It's not just about some quick foundation and a twist of mascara. In the West a bride may have her make-up professionally applied. Airbrushing is the latest make-up technique to create a flawless face. And naturally she'll need the tattoo bearing her ex-boyfriend's name hidden by a tattoo removal kit. At traditional Asian pre-wedding Mehndi parties, henna, which stains the skin, is painted over the hands and feet in flowing paisley, floral or geometric designs. More extreme are the matrimonial customs from the village of Donje Ljubinje, between Kosovo and Macedonia, where brides traditionally have their faces fully painted in pale blue and squirls of gold to ward off bad luck.

Wedding guests won't see a bride's underwear, but the groom most certainly will. It might be useful to have some help to shape the torso and hips, but does a bride really want her husband to have to wrestle her out of body-control cycling shorts on her wedding night? Today some sexy corsets look good as well as do the work. Lingerie label Agent Provocateur does an elegant waspie, or waist corset, as part of its bridal range today, and corsetry company Ender Legard makes beautiful underwear bodies, which both look elegant and smooth out the figure. And of course the saucy garter is part of many Western brides' outfits – typically worn in blue.

It used to be traditional for a bride and her bridesmaids to dress identically to confuse bad spirits who might cause the bride trouble on her wedding day. The bridesmaids sometimes even wore veils too. Somehow this feels like a wedding fad that is unlikely to make a comeback. How would the control-freak Bridezillas cope with the competition?

Right

A model poses at the Spring/ Summer 1995 Lacroix show. The ornate sleeves cleverly reveal the shoulders, while hiding the upper arms, for a soft summer look.

Left

A model strikes a pose on the catwalk during the Christian Dior couture show for Spring/Summer 2007. The delicate mille feuille layers of this skirt are quite beautiful and, made up in a soft colour, would be ideal for a bride.

Right

This dress by Giles Deacon for the label Giles was shown for Spring/ Summer 2008 at London Fashion Week. The fabric detail with its shredded leaves of silk makes this dress quite unique.

Left

Valentino made this £150,000 wedding
dress for heiress Marie-Chantal Miller
when she married Crown Prince Pavlos
of Greece in 1995. Delicate petals and
flowers picked out in beads adorned
the dress of ivory silk, but the crowning
glory is her veil. Her neat posy seems
restrained and out of place. Posies were
at their most popular in Britain during
the Victorian era, when each flower
had a meaning, and a simple bunch
of flowers between lovers could send
numerous different secret messages.

Above

Lady Sarah Armstrong-Jones marries
Daniel Chatto at St Stephen Walbrook
Church, London, in 1994. Jasper
Conran designed the bride's romantic
white silk wedding dress, as well as
the matching bridesmaids' gowns. The
dresses are simplicity itself, but the
detailing snaking down the backbone
and the romantic pink flowers bring
them to life.

Above

When legendary screen actress Rita Hayworth married Prince Aly Khan, son of the Aga Khan, in 1949 she chose a wide-brimmed hat instead of a veil. The veil for brides came back into fashion in the mid-nineteenth century, and is derived from the idea that at an arranged marriage, the bride's face should be obscured from her future husband.

Right

Star of the silver screen and fashion icon Marlene Dietrich poses for the camera. Her husky voice, legendary legs and rumoured bisexuality added to the allure that influenced fashion designers and actresses following in her Hollywood footsteps. A bride who does not want to show her upper arms might consider a dress with draped off-the-shoulder sleeves and a soft neckline which is more forgiving than a full strapless gown.

A bride's bouquet should always complement her gown. This intensely bright posy (top left) brings some colour to an all-white dress. Queen Victoria made the posy fashionable in 1860. A loose cascade bouquet (bottom left) is a romantic option for a traditionally dressed bride.

This bouquet (top right) combines a neat posy of white roses, with trailing stephanotis – a symbol of marital happiness. A white dress is the perfect backdrop for a delicate crescent-shaped bouquet (bottom right) in a bright colour.

This model (right) wears a wedding gown by French designer Christian Lacroix in 2006. The soft, sheer layers of fabric, which sit over the dress like a veil, give a soft-focus romantic effect, but it is the sharp contrast of the fabric detailing at the hem and the blue ribbon at the neckline that makes this dress a hit.

Eighteen-year-old French actress Brigitte Bardot smiles and leans her head on the shoulder of her husband, French film director Roger Vadim, in 1952. She wears white gloves and a white fur muff to keep warm at her December wedding. Flowers, embroidery, ribbons and beading can be added to a plain veil to provide interest; it is particularly effective when worn with a plain dress.

Right

Less is more. Italian actress Pier Angeli makes a beautiful bride. The elegance here is in the simplicity of her dress, with only the collar, cuffs and headpiece providing the ornamentation. Headdresses like this one were popular in the Fifties, and lace, embroidery and beading provided lavish detailing on fairytale dresses with full skirts.

The tip of the veil should finish just above or below any focal point of the dress. On the left, the elbow-length veil emphasizes the neat waistline of this Givenchy dress and complements the full skirt. Ornate dresses such as this one benefit from a plainer veil, but a simple gown often needs more ornamentation, such as a beaded or lace veil.

A piece of antique lace can make a wonderful veil, particularly when set back from the face (bottom right). The veil's colour should always match the dress, like this one (top left). Simple shoulder length veils often include

a blusher piece (bottom left) which is worn over the face, and blushers can also be combined with longer veils. For a formal wedding chapel veils (top right) fall near the floor and work well with tiaras and ornate headpieces, but for a grand dress with a train choose a trailing cathedral-length veil.

Roger Moore poses with Luisa Mattioli
after their wedding at Caxton Hall in
London in 1969. Rather then wearing
a veil, she chooses spiralling hairpieces
tipped with fabric flowers worn at the
sides of the head like the headpiece of
a Twenties bride. These complement
the fabric flowers on her dress.

Above

This 1953 bride wears a fox-fur stole
and a band of flowers in her hair
to contrast with her ornate wedding
reception gown. The gentle white
flowers help to soften the bright print.

Above

Alfonso, Prince of Asturias and eldest
son of Spain's King Alfonso, weds
a Cuban, Edelmira Sampedro-Robato,
in 1933. Headdresses of pearls and
silk flowers were fashionable at the
time, and long veils were used to
swathe tight-fitting white dresses
in a soft layer of tulle.

Right

Actress Raquel Welch and her new
husband, producer Patrick Curtis, walk
the Paris streets on 14 February 1967,
their wedding day. Her glamorous but
minimal dress is typically of the 1960s
– an era when fashionable brides wore
short child-like embroidered dresses
and lace minis.

Above

The twenty-one-year-old popstar bride
Avril Lavigne wears a Vera Wang ivory
strapless organza gown with wrapped
bodice and appliqué lace beaded skirt.
The hem and neckline were detailed
with delicately scalloped fabric. She
carried a bouquet of white roses. Her
loose hair and simple cross necklace
create a 'less is more' youthful look.

Right

Laura Parker Bowles arrives for her
wedding to Harry Lopes in 2006
in Wiltshire, England. She wears
a simple damsel dress by Robinson
Valentine with a V-neck and three-
quarter-length bell sleeves. While
her tiara and earrings are grand,
the dress is understated and detailing
on the dress is reserved for the sleeves.

In this scene from the 1969 film *The Italian Job*, the bride wears a beautiful floral headdress which tumbles over her hair like a delicate veil. Her thin white gloves finish off the summer look.

Actress Pauline Starke wears a wedding dress in the film *Love's Blindness* in 1926. She wears strings of pearls. European brides chose dresses peppered with pearls to symbolize a girl's tears – the more tears now, the less later as a wife. The ancient Greeks associated pearls with the tears of the sea nymphs, and they became symbols of a happy marriage.

A model wears a wedding dress
by Molyneux in 1946 (top left).
Her headdress of flowers delicately
suspends the veil high above her
head. Jill Esmond-Moore is Laurence
Olivier's bride in 1930 (top right).
British film actress Marjorie Hume
marries Eric Lindsey in 1933 (bottom

left). Typical Thirties headpieces
included diadems, flowers and
headdresses of stiffened tulle. Jane
Wyman's fur hat makes a discreet
reference to the veil at her 1940
wedding to Ronald Reagan
(bottom right).

Swedish-born actress Ingrid Bergman
wears a fashionable Juliet cap at her
wedding to dentist Petter Lindstrom
in 1937 (right).

Left

Natasha Henstridge stars in *Widow on the Hill* in 2005. Fur stoles and wraps are a stylish winter alternative to a summer lace jacket. Cream cashmere beaded wraps and fur muffs are other winter alternatives.

Right

A model walks the runway at the Vera Wang bridal show in New York City. A simple strapless dress can be complemented by a more ornate bolero, wrap or cover-up for the ceremony.

Above

The bride Mrs Franklin D. Roosevelt poses for the camera in 1905. She wears a stiff satin dress with shirred tulle detailing the neck and sleeves. Rose point Brussels lace, which belonged to her grandmother, covers the dress and matches her long lace veil.

Right

American film director Russ Meyer, famous for his low-budget films featuring large-breasted actresses, strikes a pose with his new wife, actress Edy Williams, in 1970. During their marriage he photographed her for *Playboy*. She has no shame in flaunting her garter. Garters were originally taken from the bride as proof that the marriage had been consummated.

This 1927 royal wedding (above) is
between the daughter of the pretender
to the French throne and a cousin of
the King of Italy. Trains can fall from
the shoulders or the waist, and some
can be detached after the ceremony to
enable dancing. A less formal option
is for the dress to be cut longer at the
back to form a train, so that the gown
simply pools out behind the bride
as she walks up the aisle.

Lady Diana Spencer's grand royal train (top right) was over seven metres long. This elegant dress with its long train is by Balmain (top left). Mabel Wisse Smit at her Netherlands wedding to Prince

Johan Friso makes a bold statement with bows in 2004 (bottom left). A model wears a wedding dress by Desses in 1953 with a fluid feminine train flowing from the shoulders (bottom right).

Left

The detailing on the veil at this 1997 Côte d'Azur wedding gives a feeling of opulence and ornament to this elegant and low-key dress.

Above

Over sixty countries have a tradition of using henna in weddings. In a non-religious ceremony, a family celebration takes place prior to marriage to adorn the bride in the home.

Left

The beautiful detailing on the back of this dress by Vera Wang takes away any need for opulent jewellery such as necklaces and earrings, and could provide a stunning back view if worn for a ceremony.

Right

Actress Carol McComas wears an evening dress with ruched sleeves and a lace sweeping skirt and bustier in 1905. A corset pulls in her waist, while the bosom is flung forward in the fashionable style of the Belle Epoque era. A garland of flowers adorns her hair.

Following page left

Fashion designer Alex Gore Browne marries JCB heir Jo Bamford in London in 2007 wearing a silk gown, which she made herself. She carries a discreet posy with trailing ribbons, a modern take on the love knot bouquets fashionable in the early twentieth century.

Following page right

American film actress Mary Pickford looks radiant in her 1920s wedding dress. By this time large bouquets had replaced the Victorian fashion for posies, and lovers knots fell in streams from a cluster of flowers. These ribbons knotted with buds and leaves influenced the bridal trend for swing flowers – blossom on thin ribbons trailing from beneath a posy.

FURTHER READING

Agins, Teri, *The End of Fashion: How Marketing Changed the Clothing Business Forever.* New York: William Morrow & Company, 1999

Barthes, Roland, *The Fashion System,* translated by Matthew Ward and Richard Howard. Berkeley: University of California Press, 1990

Baudot, François, *Fashion: The Twentieth Century.* New York: Universe, 2006

Bluttal, Steven, *Halston.* London: Phaidon, 2001

Corré, Joseph and Rees, Serena, *Agent Provocateur: A Celebration of Femininity.* London: Carlton, 1999

Cunnington, Phillis and Lucas, Catherine, *Costumes for Births, Marriages and Deaths.* London: A&C Black, 1972

Davis, Fred, *Fashion, Culture, and Identity.* Chicago: University of Chicago Press, 1992

Demornex, Jacqueline and Canino, Patricia, *Madeleine Vionnet.* Paris: Editions du Regard, 1990; London & New York: Thames & Hudson, 1991

Foster, Helen Bradley and Johnson, Donald Clay (editors), *Wedding Dress Across Cultures.* Oxford & New York: Berg, 2004

Freeman, Elizabeth, *The Wedding Complex: Forms of Belonging in Modern American Culture.* Durham, NC: Duke University Press, 2002

Haugland, Kristina, H. *Grace Kelly: Icon of Style to Royal Bride.* Philadelphia, PA: Philadelphia Museum of Art, 2006

Laver, James, *Modesty in Dress: An Inquiry into the Fundamentals of Fashion.* London: Heinemann, 1969

Lurie, Alison, *The Language of Clothes.* New York: Vintage Books, 1983

Manolo Blahnik Drawings. London & New York: Thames & Hudson, 2003

Martin, Richard and Koda, Harold, *Christian Dior.* New York: The Metropolitan Museum of Art, 1997

McDowell, Colin, *Galliano.* London: Weidenfeld & Nicolson, 1997

McDowell, Colin (editor), *The Pimlico Companion to Fashion.* London: Pimlico, 1998

Peacock, John, *The Complete Fashion Sourcebook.* London & New York: Thames & Hudson, 2005

Richards, Melissa, *Chanel: Key Collections.* London: Hamlyn, 2000

Steele, Valerie, *Fifty Years of Fashion: New Look to Now.* New Haven, CT: Yale University Press, 2000

Wilcox, Claire (editor), *The Golden Age of Couture: Paris and London 1947–57.* London & New York: V&A Publications, 2007

Woodall, Trinny and Constantine, Susannah, *What Not to Wear.* London: Weidenfeld & Nicolson, 2004

Worsley, Harriet, *Classics of Fashion.* London: Brown Reference Group, 2002

Worsley, Harriet, *Decades of Fashion.* Cologne: Könemann, 2000

PICTURE CREDITS

AKG Images / Erich Lessing 223

Big Pictures 132 / Malibu Media 250

Bridgeman © The Bridgeman Art Library 148

Camera Press / Bassano 144 / Simon Grosset 239 / R. Stonehouse 127

Corbis / Michel Arnaud 75, 234 / Bettmann 33, 53, 57, 70, 107,135, 138, 167, 168, 170, 211, 232, 262, 266, 267, 278, 306 / Sunset Boulevard 74 / Stephane Cardinale 246, 288 (TL) / Conde Nast 151 / Alain Dejean 271 / Henry Diltz 177 / Mitchell Gerber 59 / Cynthia Hart Designer 142 / Hulton-Deutsch Collection 293 (TL) 62 / Andanson James 310 / Karen Kasmauski 197 / Brooks Kraft 36 / Andrew Lichtenstein 176 / Andrew Murray 190 / Genevieve Naylor 34, 292, 302 (TL), 309 (BR,TL) / Michael Nicholson 129 / Thierry Orban 102, 281 / Norman Parkinson 123 / Eric Robert 222 / Sygma 197 / Pierre Vauthey 106

Getty 208 / AFP 92, 286, 289, 297 / Arif Ali 185 / Allan 76 / Tengku Bahar 195 / Bryan Bedder 117, 305, 312 / Dave M. Benett 202, 228 / Jack Benton 227 / Jack Birns 219 / Tim Boxer 237 / Vince Bucci 298 / Joe Buissink 7 / Central Press 68, 215, 221, 294 / Charles / New York Times Co. 22 / China Photos 196 / E. Dean 113 / Sahm Doherty 191 / Francois Durand 159 / Frank Edwards 307 / Evening Standard 61 / Express 54, 230 / Jayne Fincher 309 / Ron Galella 44 / General Photographic Agency 301 / Tim Graham 284, 285 / Francois Guillot 14 / Dirck Halstead 82 / Bert Hardy 13, 220 (BL) / Frazer Harrison 251 / Dave Hogan 32, 48 / Stan Honda 260 / Hulton 60, 93, 131, 174, 240, 241, 296 / Anwar Hussein 17, 238 / Imagno / Austrian Archives 218 / isifa 90 / Chris Jackson 299 / Dmitri Kessel 31 / Keystone 42 , 63,124, 203, 207, 244, 248 (TL) / John Kobal Foundation 101 / Peter Kramer 181 / Lisa Larsen 220 (ML) / Lavandeira Jr 156 / Eric Liebowitz 235 / William Lovelace 233 (TR) / Arnaldo Magnani 23 / Mark Mainz 162 / Salah Malkawi 192 / George Marks 212 / Thomas D. Mcavoy 9 / Arnaldo Magnani 46 / Kevin Mazur 27 / Chris Moore 189, 282 /

Morgan Collection 236 / Andy Nelson 273 / Sam Panthaky 256 / Tony Perkins 149 / John Phillips 108 / George Pimentel 141 / Michel Porro 175 / Karl Prouse 283 / Thomas Rabsch 255 / RDA 290 / Fred Ramage 28 / Cesar Rangel 24 / Jack Robinson 150 / Michael Rougier 295 / Eric Ryan 269 / Sasha 73, 302 (TR, BL) / Pascal Le Segretain 136, 288 (TR), 293 (BR) / Noah Seelam 272 / Peter Stackpole 72 / Syndication International 77 / Three Lions 220 (TL) / Topical Press Agency 139 / Pierre Verdy 94, 259 / Bruno Vincent 247 / Roger Viollet Collection 199 / Julian Wasser 134 / Kevin Winter 86 / Toru Yamanaka 288 (BR)

Goff Photos / Davidson 20, 314 / Queen 216, 277 Courtesy Hello! Magazine 186, 187

Helnwein / Odessy Barbu, © Studio Helnwein 261

Kobal Collection 18, 21, 25, 26, 67, 88, 104, 112, 200, 287, 291, 300, 302 (BR), 304 / Columbia 105 / Elmer Fryer 114 / George Hurrell 96 / MGM 111 / First National / Warner Bros 81 / Paramount 41, 89, 155 / RKO 40 / Clarence Sinclair 97 / 20th Century Fox 91 / Warner Bros 99

Pacific Coast News / Victoria Stewart 143

PA Photos / Joerg Carstensen 242 / Christophe Ena 38 / Courtesy Oscar de la Renta / Dan & Corina Lecca / Brides Magazine

Reuters 233 (BR) / Jack Dabaghian 166 / Amit Dave 194 /Muhammad Hamed 188 / Tientan Ling 311 / Yuriko Nakao 161 / Jean-Paul Pelissier 268 / Ognen Teofilovski 184 / Robin Utrecht 309 (BL) / Philippe Wojazer 110

Rex / 98, 293 (TR) / Brendan Beirne 116 / Peter Brooker 264 / Charbonneau 58/ Everett Collection 233 (BL), 248 (TR, BR), 249, 263 / David Fisher 243 / David Hartley 147 / Keystone USA 100 / Henry Lamb /BEI 45 / Jon Lyons 71 / Brian Moody 165 / Alex Oliveira 173 / Olycom SPA 270 / Nick Randall 171 / Jukka Ritola 164 / Sipa Press 84, 133, 198, 214, 217, 248 (BL) / SNAP 69 /

UMDADC 35 / Roger Viollet 118 / Steve Wood 172 / Richard Young 85, 103

Superstock 146

© Tate, London 2008 137

Topfoto 128, 245, 293 (BL) / UPP 288 (BL)

V&A Images / Victoria & Albert Museum / Cecil Beaton 30 / John French 49 / after Sir George Hayter 37 / Lady Hawarden 39 / Layfayette 43, 140 / Kind permission of Zandra Rhodes 130

Courtesy of Vionnet / Nefis Dhab 119

Courtesy of Amanda Wakeley 87

INDEX

Page numbers in bold refer to main text entries.